# MORAL FIBER

# MORAL FIBER

### AWAKENING

### CORPORATE

### CONSCIOUSNESS

SHAWN VIJ

MORAL FIBER

*Awakening Corporate Consciousness*

ISBN    978-1-61961-629-5 *Hardcover*

978-1-61961-630-1 *Paperback*

978-1-61961-631-8 *Ebook*

LIONCREST
PUBLISHING

TO MY BELOVED DAUGHTER

# CONTENTS

——

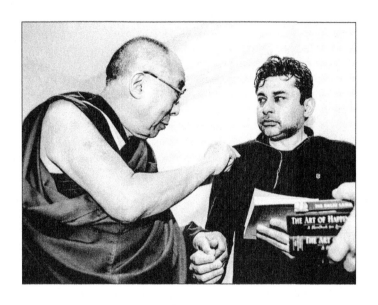

"It is in everybody's interest to seek those [actions]
that lead to happiness and avoid those which
lead to suffering. And because our interests
are inextricably linked, we are compelled to
accept ethics as the indispensable interface
between my desire to be happy and yours."

HIS HOLINESS THE DALAI LAMA

THE DALAI LAMA

# FOREWORD

The world faces many complex problems—problems of corruption, environment, politics, and so on. Despite enormous development in material wealth and comfort, people everywhere are feeling less happy and more stressed.

The problems that we see in the world today almost always indicate a failure of moral ethics and inner values, such as love and compassion. At every level, we see a lack of self–discipline. The 2008 global economic crisis whose repercussions are still felt around the world is a clear example of how unbridled greed on the part of a few can adversely affect the lives of millions. As long as we are unable to pay equal importance to inner moral values and ethics as we do to material development, the world will continue to face such problems into the future. That is why, for many years, I have been making concerted effort to promote inner human values everywhere I go.

I am happy to learn that Shawn Vij, who has extensive background in corporate business, shares my concern for these issues, and has written this book, *Moral Fiber,* to help more people learn how to incorporate universal moral values and secular ethics into our education system as well as in corporate business. Inspired by his own experiences as well as that of other key leaders in business and leading academia, he shares with us how compassion, gratitude and wisdom opens our inner door, unlocking a more purposeful life and career.

My congratulations and best wishes to Shawn Vij for writing this book and for its success. I have no doubt that his message will be well-received by his readership.

March 15, 2017

# FOREWORD

## BY HIS HOLINESS
## THE DALAI LAMA

---

The world faces many complex problems—problems of corruption, environment, politics, and so on. Despite enormous development in material wealth and comfort, people everywhere are feeling less happy and more stressed.

The problems that we see in the world today almost always indicate a failure of moral ethics and inner values, such as love and compassion. At every level, we see a lack of self-discipline. The 2008 global economic crisis whose repercussions are still felt around the world is a clear example of how unbridled greed on the part of a few can adversely affect the lives of millions. As long as we are unable to pay equal importance to inner moral values and ethics as we do to material development, the world will continue to face such problems into the future. That is why, for many years, I have been making concerted effort to promote inner human values everywhere I go.

I am happy to learn that Shawn Vij, who has extensive background in corporate business, shares my concern for these issues, and has written this book, *Moral Fiber*, to help more people learn how to incorporate universal moral values and secular ethics into our education system as well as in corporate business. Inspired by his own experiences as well as that of other key leaders in business and leading academia, he shares with us how compassion, gratitude and wisdom opens our inner door, unlocking a more purposeful life and career.

My congratulations and best wishes to Shawn Vij for writing this book and for its success. I have no doubt that his message will be well-received by his readership.

— HIS HOLINESS THE DALAI LAMA

# AUTHOR'S NOTE

---

Since writing this book, I couldn't have predicted the dramatic turn of events that would arise while I worked on *Moral Fiber*. Like many, I've watched as the United States has seemed to grow more divisive. Race, religion, politics, ethnicity, environmental protection, the list of issues and reasons for people to choose sides seems endless.

We're living during a time where some of us may question whether there is a place, or need, for values like I've discussed in *Moral Fiber*. I argue there is. There is an opportunity for us all to act on the one thing that unites humanity: our common core values.

Focusing on the simple acts of respect, kindness, fairness and compassion reminds each of us of who we are, who we should be, and who we can be. This is our natural state as human beings. This natural state still requires a daily discipline of knowing and acting on our values—of acting on our moral fiber. It is my sincerest wish that this book will remind readers of what brings us together, rather than what sets us apart.

# PREFACE

———

Stillness surrounded me as I sat on the edge of a weathered couch in the circular lobby of a downtown San Jose, California, hotel. I felt the tear and thread of the cloth as my hand clutched the armrest. It was February 24, 2014. The time was 7:32 a.m., and the only people around me were two hotel receptionists and a handful of diplomatic security service agents.

The aroma of fresh coffee filled the air while the chanting of protestors outside echoed through the empty halls and arched ceilings of the lobby. I was anxious. My heart pounded with the sense that my life, in a moment, was about to change. Sitting there on the couch, I knew there was a reason—one I could not explain—for everything that I had become, and everything I was going to be.

Suddenly, two security men in navy suits approached me and my brother, Dave who was seated next to me. They asked for our names and identification before escorting us into an old cargo elevator that carried me and my anxiety up fifteen floors.

As the doors slowly opened, I began to see, for the first time, my purpose in life.

The hallway was filled with people in maroon robes, and my mind started to crawl into equanimity. I felt detached from everyone and everything around me, as I bowed my head and walked toward His Holiness the Dalai Lama.

The noises around me silenced, and each step toward His Holiness reinforced my calling. Tears welled in my eyes as I dropped to my knees before him to touch his feet.

It was at this very moment, I sought salvation. I was at a place in my life where everything that had defined me shattered. I had stopped taking care of my health, my job was toxic, the future of my marriage was uncertain, and I had slowly distanced myself from my family and friends. I became crippled and found myself in an environment full of doubt and uncertainty. The pain was so strong it had fractured my soul.

The Dalai Lama gently reached down and lifted me with his hands. He pulled me close to him.

His eyes were soft as he gazed at me while I shared with him my story. In that moment, it was as though he could feel the cause of all my suffering.

"I don't know why, but I feel so angry," I revealed.

"The only way to get past anger is to have compassion," he told me.

"I don't know if I have that right now," I confessed.

"You're getting blinded by the anger. It will come."

The Dalai Lama suggested I read, *A Guide to the Bodhisattva's Way of Life*, which contain practices or disciplines someone would use to attain self-realization. He said I should pay close attention to chapters six, seven, and nine, especially the last.

"What's chapter nine?" I asked.

"Chapter nine is on wisdom. Wisdom will help you. Wisdom will be your guide."

"Wisdom will be my guide to what?" I wondered out loud.

"Wisdom will be the guide to your happiness," he said matter-of-factly.

That was hard for me to believe. I didn't feel happy, and I doubted if I ever would. Truthfully, what was happiness? What did the word mean? As we spoke, a constant smile graced his face. He never lost eye contact with me nor did he drop my hand from his. Throughout our conversation, security guards, monks, diplomats, and my brother gathered around us, watching, listening, and fully engaged as if they were experiencing my pain with me.

And through all the hurt that surged, I was able to find a place of inner peace.

As our time together ended, His Holiness leaned close to me, so close only I could hear what he whispered in my ear.

"Your enemy is your greatest teacher. And your greatest enemy is in you."

I was in awe of this man.

"You are my master," I said reverently, but he furrowed his brow at my comment and in a rather scolding tone, admonished me.

"*You* are your own master."

# INTRODUCTION

## THE JOURNEY BEGINS

———

My first meeting with His Holiness was a spiritual encounter. I had never felt so much sadness and happiness at the same time. It was as though an awakening occurred. After that experience, I realized I had a greater calling for me in my life. For more than twenty-five years, I worked as a senior business leader and consultant tasked with launching new products, managing million-dollar relationships, and building high-performing teams for major Fortune 100 companies. But after countless successes, I found myself being asked to compromise who I was and what I valued personally and professionally.

Thankfully, the Dalai Lama opened an inner door for

me. Our first encounter left me thirsty for knowledge on Buddhism, so I read anything and everything I could find online and in books. Taking a secular approach with Buddhist philosophy, I started to see myself, my relationships, and my career differently. I began to self-reflect more deeply, and I realized for most of my life that I had overreacted to situations, to people, and to environments.

Even more concerning to me was the realization that as I advanced in my career, I was repeatedly asked to distance myself from my core values such as fairness, respect, compassion, and honesty—the same values that had defined me as a person since I was a child.

For most of my career, I felt trapped by the circumstances and toxic work environments I encountered. From the moment I began in the corporate world, I faced situations and people that challenged my values. At times, I played the yes-man and was influenced by pernicious behavior of others and by corporate politics. Despite my better judgment, I did what I was told and never pushed back or questioned why.

I lived by the mantra "It's not personal; it's just business."

Like many men and women, I was afraid of the repercussions if I didn't mold myself to fit the environments that I worked in. I feared losing my position, power, and future opportunities to rise through the ranks if I bucked the system. Similar to many senior business leaders, I let my lifestyle shackle me.

It was as though everyone was caught in a vicious cycle of toxic actions—of actions taken in ignorance, anger, and fear—because of misplaced values.

Once I became aware of what was happening to me, I saw it happening everywhere to everyone. Up and down the corridors of my office and within the walls of numerous corporations, I was shocked by what I witnessed and learned. Everywhere I turned, I watched people across the organization, from front-line employees to recent MBA graduates, to middle managers, to executives, toil away in toxic work environments that negatively affected and influenced them.

I watched as people were deceived, betrayed, belittled, ignored, lied to, and treated disrespectfully by leaders, superiors, managers, coworkers, and subordinates. I was stunned to witness so many people compromising their values at the altar of financial rewards, cash bonuses, and fancy job titles. Yet, despite their material successes, when I looked closely, I saw how painfully unhappy, discontent, and purposeless most of them were.

The worst part was, these behaviors negatively impacted business productivity, investment decisions, employee attrition, and the well-being of everyone in the office.

That's when the seed for this book was planted.

I'd had enough of watching countless people needlessly suffering, compromising their values for the sake of the dollar, and feeling trapped in toxic environments. I wanted to help others, like myself, be successful in business without having to compromise their values.

All of us can quickly rattle off companies with extremely toxic environments that yield high profit margins. Are these companies sustainable, though? What's the true business cost, social impact, and effect on employee well-being that happens in these destructive environments?

In my experience, toxic environments lead to rampant unhappiness, stifled creativity, limited innovation, loss of top talent, and an erosion of personal values.

A positive environment, on the other hand, generates remarkable results. Teams and companies have higher productivity levels, happiness, team unity, loyalty, and enhanced creativity and innovation. These teams and companies also attract some of the best talent. Perhaps more importantly, people stay true to themselves and rarely compromise their values in positive environments.

Our world needs more teams and companies that not only thrive in creating wealth and growing the business, but also do it while treating people with dignity, respect, and compassion. Our world, especially our corporate environment, needs to reflect our own humanity.

So how do we act on our values? How do we begin to change the corporate drywall, attitude, and culture? How do we change toxic environments, while remaining true to ourselves?

The answer lies within each of us. Our own capacity and willingness to change becomes our greatest strength or weakness. It is in the shadows we form and cast that influence the people and environment around us. It is at the individual level where our power to alter our experiences rests. While alone we may not be able to reshape the company, we can collectively, if each of us does our part.

This is accomplished when we build and use what I call our moral fiber. Our moral fiber is the daily practice of *knowing* and *acting* on our core values that brings about this evolution and growth within ourselves and our environments. That is the focus of this book.

Our moral fiber is like a muscular tissue that keeps us attuned to our innate core values and protected against the influence of toxic environments, situations, and people. To strengthen our moral fiber, we first need to recognize our core values, such as fairness, respect, compassion, and honesty, and then we must genuinely act on them daily. The more we practice acting on our values despite challenging experiences, the stronger our moral fiber becomes. Eventually, we find ourselves in a place where we never compromise on our values no matter the pressure from the environment, our colleagues, subordinates, and leaders.

In turn, acting on our core values strikes a chord in the people around us, and we begin to influence our coworkers, managers, customers, and business partners in a constructive way.

Since I've strengthened my moral fiber, my life has dramatically changed, personally and professionally. I'm happier and more engaged in my work, and I'm more mindful and calm when making business decisions. While I still navigate through some very toxic environments and people, I'm no longer influenced by them. Today, I'm more aware of my boss, team, customers, and direct reports, *and* how my actions impact their actions.

Most importantly, I'm more aware of myself.

It's as though I've awoken a consciousness within, and I've discovered a greater sense of purpose in my life and work. I act with more compassion, forgiveness, wisdom, and patience. I've become a positive influence and role model to those around me and my environment instead of feeding into the toxic environment. And whereas I once felt forced to choose between advancing and protecting my career versus treating people with compassion and respect, today I'm doing both. I'm thriving by driving significant business outcomes for my company while simultaneously acting on my values.

As the Dalai Lama says, "Establishing binding ethical principles is possible when we take as our starting point the observations that we all desire happiness and not to suffer. We have no means of discriminating between right and wrong if we do not take into account others' feelings, others' suffering."[1]

In a way, I now aspire to achieve a state of eudaemonia, a classical Greek word meaning *happiness*. According to Aristotle, eudaemonia is constituted not by honor, wealth, or power, but by rational activity in accordance with virtue over a complete life, better described today as productive self-actualization. It is a moral philosophy that defines right action which leads to the "well-being" of the individual.

1   The Dalai Lama, *Ethics for the New Millennium* (Penguin, 2001), 49.

Attaining eudaemonia, means we must question the choices we make, especially at the office. I believe that by knowing and practicing our common core values (our moral fiber) in our everyday activities that we can exercise practical wisdom in resolving any conflict or dilemma that arises, which will allow each of us to experience eudaemonia.

This book is my attempt to awaken our core values so we can better elevate, navigate, and positively impact toxic environments. It is everyone's right, no matter their age or position, to experience greater happiness and purpose in their lives while succeeding professionally. This book is for the following:

- Those who feel trapped in their job
- Those who are forced to compromise their values at the office
- Those who agonize over becoming someone they are not
- Those who are ambushed in corporate politics or cast aside
- Those who seek to be the "conscious" change agent at the office
- Those who seek a greater purpose in their professional lives

In the following pages, I share with you the journey that I took from being the man who said, "It's not personal; it's just business," to becoming the man who says, "It's business *and* it's always personal." Woven throughout the book are tips, tools, and tales, as well as a little insight and inspiration on how we can return to our core values.

I share with you my own experiences and observations as well as those from global business leaders, leading academia, and researchers on the following:

- ⚬ What is really happening in our offices
- ⚬ How we crush our souls by compromising our values
- ⚬ How to identify the four most damaging behaviors in organizations
- ⚬ How to rediscover and act on our core values through self-awareness
- ⚬ How to strengthen our moral fiber through daily practice of our values
- ⚬ How to successfully navigate and positively influence toxic environments

His Holiness the Dalai Lama told me that I'm my own master. He was right; I am. But so are you. No matter where you find yourself—whether you're an executive caught in a compromising situation or environment, a newly minted MBA graduate about to embark on a business career, or a barista working at a local coffee shop—you have the choice to rediscover and act on your values to create a happier, more purpose-driven, more engaged work life.

As each of us journey through our careers, we will face many decisions that will define who we become. At times, we will face toxic environments, people, and situations that test our values. However, it is in our moral fiber, the daily practice of *knowing* and *acting* on our core values, that we will awaken our consciousness and give greater purpose to our lives and the organizations we work for.

CHAPTER 1

# CRUSHING MY SOUL

———

SAKKAYADITTHI *DEF*. WRONG VIEW OF SELF

As I emerged from the underground subway onto Market Street, I felt the ocean breeze against my face as the smell of eucalyptus lifted my thoughts. I walked with my ego soaring through the streets of San Francisco to my office. I was in the global epicenter at the cross streets of technology and innovation. At thirty-one years old, the feeling of power and control inspired me.

Pushing my way through the corporate stream of workers, I headed toward my office with my Americano from Peet's Coffee gripped in one hand and a laptop bag dangling off the opposite shoulder. Casually dressed in a button-up jean shirt, loosely tucked into my brown khakis and with the sleeves rolled to my elbows, I walked with my thoughts drifting to the night before, when my baby girl uttered the word *daddy* for the first time.

Smiling to that memory, I climbed to the seventeenth floor, and with a burst of positive energy, I entered my cubicle. I slipped my laptop into the docking station and checked my calendar as photos of my family and affirmations of "Teamwork" and "Loyalty" surrounded my desk. Grabbing my things, I strolled to the corner conference room to start my first meeting of the day.

Walking in, I found my manager, two of her colleagues, and my project team discussing key business requirements for the next product we were about to launch. Immediately, I noticed something was different—something was off. No one made eye contact with me, said hello, or acknowledged my existence. Even my manager, Carrie, looked away from me. *Maybe they're too deep in discussion,* I thought and shrugged it off.

ঽ ঽ ঽ

I never understood why I was tapped for my role on the team. I was the product management guy, but Carrie had me acting as the accountant, managing the profit and loss for our multimillion-dollar project. Our company received a huge financial investment from a number of clients, and my team was to launch a new product from scratch. I was charged with handling the finances, from reviewing the investments made on our project to how we spent the money. When I asked Carrie why she chose me for this responsibility, she nonchalantly said she needed someone she could trust in this position.

From the start, something seemed wrong with the numbers. We had brought on consultants, but I didn't know who they were. Their names just showed up on the books with significant charges in the range of $30,000 to $40,000 per month. At first, I didn't say anything. But as the months passed and more charges were added, I couldn't keep my unease to myself.

I brought my concerns to Carrie, who was highly regarded in the company as a senior executive with more than twenty years of experience within the industry. Plus, I trusted her. She told me not worry about the charges, that things were moving the way they should and to focus on my work.

I did as she said, except the nagging feeling that something was off with the balance sheet wouldn't go away. I went to Carrie again, but this time, her response was shorter and curter to me. So I tried a different tactic and took my concerns to another senior executive who suggested I raise the issue with someone above my boss.

That advice made sense, but I remember wondering how I could go above her without having it ricochet back onto me, jeopardizing my job. I needed that position. I had a young family, and my wife and I had recently relocated to the Bay Area. We were starting to settle and build a life there. We had purchased our first home and gone into extreme debt to make it a reality. Moreover, we had a nine-month-old baby girl whom we needed to take care of.

Turns out, I didn't have to orchestrate a conversation with a senior leader. I just needed to be in the right place at the right time. I was eating lunch in the cafeteria one day when I spotted an old colleague sitting with the chief financial officer (CFO) of the company. I stared at them from across the room, frantically wondering what I should do. Should I say something about the situation? Was my hunch about the books worth risking my career and my family?

Yes, yes, it was.

It was my moment to act on my values and to do what I thought was the right thing. I slowly rose and walked toward my colleague and the CFO. As I drew closer to their table, I noticed an open seat. *This is it*, I said to myself. *I'm going to sit and tell them everything.* My colleague looked up and we locked eyes.

"Hi, Shawn." He nodded an inviting hello.

"Hey," I whispered.

And then...

I kept walking.

At the last moment, I couldn't do it. Everything in my life— my daughter, my home, the beginning of a new life in a new city—everything felt too big, too important for me to risk. I had a moment, a chance, to act on my values, but I punted because I was scared of the consequences on my life.

A few weeks after the cafeteria incident, I tried once more to reach out to Carrie for clarity and insight. I couldn't let it go. I told her the finance team had questions and were asking to review the balance sheet.

But for a third time, my questions were ignored.

ૐ ૐ ૐ

After the odd encounter in the conference room, when I found my team and boss refused to look me in the eye, I returned to my cubicle. The morning dragged on. I couldn't shake the uneasiness that pulsed through me as I wondered why my team and boss had acted strangely toward me. Suddenly, my office phone rang. It was Carrie. She asked me to come into her manager's office. With my stomach twisted into knots, I walked into Dan's corner office overlooking the Golden Gate Bridge. My eyes latched on to an old beat-up leather bomber jacket hanging on a loose hook on the side wall. It was Dan's jacket, but Dan wasn't in the room.

Carrie and Jessica, from Human Resources, were the only ones present. Jessica began talking as a chill crept over me. Her voice became distant, and all that I heard were the words, "Shawn, this will be your last day. Your services are no longer needed."

I was stunned. My stomach tore apart and my hands shook so badly that I had to wedge them between my thighs and the chair. My world was tipping and whirling out of control. I fixed my gaze upon Dan's old beat-up bomber jacket on the loose hook as though it were an anchor that could ground me.

"Why?" I turned to Carrie. She didn't respond.

"What about a severance package?" I asked her. No response either.

"You know my wife and I just had a baby girl, right?" I pleaded. No response.

"You know we just bought a house, right?" I countered. No response.

"Can I take a different job with the company?" I urged, grasping at anything to keep my young family afloat. No response.

I peppered Carrie with questions and statements, but she remained silent through it all. She didn't care and hardly said anything to me. Everything about my termination was mechanical. There was no, "Shawn, we're sorry to have to do this," no explanation as to why I was being let go. I couldn't understand why this was happening, not when I'd received outstanding reviews and accolades as the best team player and most innovative on my team. In my years with the company, Carrie had even shared with colleagues that I was like a son to her.

As the meeting drew to a close, there was nothing left to say. I was told to leave immediately, but I sat there staring at Carrie, watching her makeup slide down her face as tears tugged her eyes closed.

"It's not personal, Shawn; it's just business," she finally said as she wiped her eyes with a red scarf.

Later, I learned that my termination was in fact the result of the questions I raised about the balance sheet. Unbeknown to me, my line of inquiry had placed a great deal of attention on Carrie and the team. I had identified things that were out of the norm and potentially unethical. My discovery had become a rumor, and she had to stop it. Months later and long after I had joined another company, news of a scandal broke. My suspicions were proven correct, and Carrie, along with most of my old team, was let go.

But it was of little solace to me.

## "IT'S NOT PERSONAL; IT'S JUST BUSINESS"

*Ten years later...*

The wheel hatch opened, and the cabin pressure increased as we began our descent to the most industrialized island on earth: Japan. It was 5:00 p.m., and I'd just landed in Narita. Waiting for me outside of customs were two of my employees. They rushed me to the first-class train service that would carry me into downtown Tokyo where I had a dinner meeting with the vice-president of a global multibillion-dollar company.

Sitting in the bullet train, I sipped a Coca-Cola as my employees briefed me on every detail of my impending meeting as well as the agenda for the week. Before dinner, I went to freshen up at my usual suite at the InterContinental Tokyo. I knew this place well, as I traveled to Japan frequently. When I walked into my room, I immediately spotted my regular luxuries: a fruit plate, wine, chocolates, a card from the local office welcoming me, and hotel representatives waiting to greet me.

As a general manager for a global team at one of the world's largest companies, my role commanded respect wherever I went.

As our cocktails arrived, I only half listened to the vice-president ramble on about how we needed to co-invest on a new project in an emerging market. Glancing around the room, I caught the profile of a tall, beautiful Japanese hostess greeting guests at their tables; I noticed her infectious smile. As I looked around at all the diners, I thought to myself, I'd made it. There I was sitting at one of the finest five-star restaurants in the world, drinking the oldest scotch, eating the highest-quality sushi, and talking to one of the top executives in the world.

It had been a long ten years since my eyes fixated on that beat-up bomber jacket in the corner office overlooking the

Golden Gate Bridge—ten long years since that infamous day when Carrie let me go. And since that fateful day, every single action and decision I made was to ensure I would never have to look at my daughter with fear and worry again.

I wish I could tell you that the lesson learned after being terminated was that I should have gone to the CFO with my concerns immediately. I wish I could tell you that moment was a turning point, when I vowed to always act on my core values. But I can't tell you that because I took a completely different lesson from that experience.

Instead of walking toward my core values, I blindly veered away from them.

I vowed as a new father to never allow myself to be placed in a similar situation. Never again would I allow my ability to care and provide for my daughter to be jeopardized. I saw how Carrie behaved, how she fired someone she considered to be like a son to her, in order to protect her domain. If she acted this way, then I had to if it meant protecting and advancing my career. As a result, I became more cutthroat, like Carrie and all the other countless leaders and executives I worked with.

"It's not personal, Shawn; it's just business," Carrie had said to me.

If that's what worked for her, then I vowed I would use that formula, too.

By the time I was sitting in Japan, in one of the finest restaurants in the world, my salary, title, and job wielded me incredible influence and power. From ringing the opening bell with my team at NASDAQ to managing a global multimillion-dollar business, I had established a career many people envied. I had the beautiful family, large home, designer suits, and a nice salary. Yet, I still wanted more. It was like I was climbing the Matterhorn, a mountain in the Swiss Alps, and I had to make it to the top. As I rose higher, I saw others like me. Some cut their ropes, while others fueled their ascent with anger and greed. I watched friends become enemies and careers sabotaged for the sake of titles, money, and power.

The higher I climbed, the more breathtaking the views and the more endless the rewards. Career advancement became a game of chutes and ladders, and losing wasn't an option for me. I welcomed the game and danced politics with the corporate elite. Like Carrie and many corporate executives, I replayed the mantra, "It's not personal; it's just business," over and over to justify my actions.

Still, in some quiet moments, I felt conflicted over my behaviors. The line "It's not personal; it's just business," pulled at me. I wanted to be true to myself—and often I was. But in many situations, it felt like an uphill battle to act authentically. So many people in the corporate world, up and down the ladder, play vicious games to advance their own business agendas and careers. And there were times when I felt that I had no choice but to concede just to survive.

I remember one time I was managing a team, and one young man, Haseem, fresh from his MBA program, wanted to transition to another office. This was about halfway through our project. He had an opportunity to take an assignment cross-country. I didn't want to see him go, but it was a great opportunity for him professionally and personally as his fiancée lived in New York City.

I gave him a greenlight, but I needed to inform the project manager, Deborah. I went to her with the situation, saying I supported his move. But Deborah didn't because of a personal sacrifice she had made in her career earlier. Deborah was in a very similar situation as Haseem years prior, and her manager didn't approve her transfer so that she could be near her boyfriend. This negative emotion reemerged in Deborah and she couldn't detach from it. I pushed back on her and said I was going to let him go to

New York, and that I was only doing her the courtesy of letting her know. I had no idea that she would go above me to our manager. Our manager sided with her—they were personal friends—and Haseem's request for transfer was denied.

When the project was finished, we had to rate all team members on a scale of one to five with five being the highest and one being the lowest. I thought Haseem did a fantastic job and made a huge sacrifice to stay. I gave him a five, but Deborah disagreed and said he deserved a one. That ranking was wrong. Nothing Haseem did warranted that low score and it would only hurt him professionally. I went to our manager, who told me to let it go, that he wasn't worth fighting for.

I was ashamed to work at this company. I was belittled, and my boss chose to look the other way, allowing her friend's personal pride to yield even greater negativity on the team. So I did the only thing that made any sense to me.

I quit.

I refused to be a party to such disrespectful and dishonest behavior.

But you can never really leave these situations or people behind you.

Unfortunately, the number of challenging people and environments increased dramatically throughout my career. Most of the time, I did my best to avoid them, praying the problems would disappear. But there were some situations that no one can avoid.

From watching employees get mistreated to seeing managers ambush others to advance their own careers, I found myself in situation after situation where my values were tested. Sometimes I took a strong stand for what I valued, such as when I quit the company over what I believe was poor treatment of my direct report, and other times, I let the toxic environment or people influence my decisions and actions.

When I think back to earlier moments in my career, I'm almost horrified because I realize now that I was numb, even senseless, to what was happening around me. I stopped feeling or recognizing how people treated me, and how I behaved toward others, too.

The hallways of excessive anger, greed, and ignorance (which I will go into later in the book) overwhelmed me. I had blindfolded myself to shield me from the toxins that surrounded me. I stopped seeing and sensing when I was caught in an ethical dilemma that tested my values.

In every situation, I just thought I was right. I always found some way to justify my actions. I lived by the mantra "It's not personal; it's just business."

Psychologists say continuous exposure to this type of repetitive behavior can cause "psychic numbing,"[1] which leads us to rationalize our thoughts and actions. This is what happened to me, and as a result, I not only deceived myself, but I also silenced my *inner voice*. This form of self-deception is "the root of ethical fading,"[2] argue Professors Ann Tenbrunsel and David Messick in their paper "Ethical Fading: The Role of Self-Deception in Unethical Behavior."

They explain that ethical fading is the "process by which the moral colors of an ethical decision fade into bleached hues that are void of moral implications."[3] Ethical fading, as they contend, happens after we've become "ethically numb."

"Repeated exposures to ethical dilemmas may produce a

---

1   Ann E. Tenbrunsel and David M. Messick, "Ethical Fading: The Role of Self-Deception in Unethical Behavior," *Social Justice Research* 17, no. 2 (2004): 228.

2   Ibid.

3   Ibid.

form of ethical numbing in which self-proof is diminished through repeated exposures,"[4] they write. "When this occurs, we may be less likely to see the 'ethical' in the dilemma, and hence engage in more unreflective and potentially more unethical behavior."[5]

This ethical numbing is exactly what happened to me, and I'd argue, what's gripped millions of men and women working in the corporate world.

When I sat in that five-star restaurant in Japan, I truly believed I had arrived. Yes, I found myself conflicted in some situations, but everything I had done, and was doing, was for my family. My sole purpose was to ensure I would never find myself in a situation where I had to worry about providing for my family again. My long-term intentions were good and pure.

It wasn't until soon after I met with the Dalai Lama that I saw clearly what had happened to me: that in my quest to provide and care for myself and my family, I had deceived myself. I believed how most businesspeople acted was fine. I believed "It's not personal; it's only business" was the right mantra to live by when, in fact, it wasn't.

---

4  Ibid.

5  Ibid.

Not once during my professional career did I contemplate the true cost on my life that resulted from my unconscious reshaping of certain values.

That true cost was I had crushed my soul.

It took a personal and professional hardship before I understood that I could succeed in business while staying true to myself and my core values. Now, this book isn't meant to create a crisis in your life in order to prompt you to know and act on your core values. It's also not my intention to create a crisis that leads you to quit your job or to avoid the corporate world altogether. My intention with this book is to show you that no matter how toxic the environment or the people around you are, you can succeed in business while embracing your values. You don't have to crush your soul or have your values fade in order to have a thriving career.

You can choose a different path. You can succeed by being true to yourself, and I'm going to show you how. The first step is recognizing where our values come from and what triggers them to potentially fade. In the next chapter, I'm going to show you what's really at the root cause of this problem.

CHAPTER 2

# CAGING OURSELVES

———

SAMSARA *DEF.* PERPETUAL WANDERING

The year was 1988. The US postage stamp was $0.24, a gallon of milk cost $1.89, a movie ticket was $3.50, and a gallon of gas was $0.91. The Iran–Iraq War had ended, a new drug called crack appeared in the United States, the movie *Rain Man* made its debut, and the Irish rock band U2 owned the charts.

The ice on the driver side window slowly melted as we sat idling in a 1978 Fairmont station wagon. Parked in my friend's driveway, we waited for the heat to kick on and our nerves to calm before heading back to college after a long weekend home in Michigan. As the snow steadily fell, my five friends and I crammed ourselves into the old wagon with wood paneling on the sides. The snowstorm raged around us turning our ten-hour journey back to school into a dark and dangerous trek across narrow and icy roads.

Our conversation turned from music selection—Beatles or Def Leopard—to whether we should find a hotel or continue driving at fifteen miles per hour. It was midnight and half of the guys wanted to continue—we had midterm exams the next day—while the rest wanted to stop. We argued for an hour until we came upon a family of five, stranded on the side of a hill, their car broken. We were in the Upper Peninsula of Michigan, a remote, secluded corridor of the state with little but forest for at least fifty miles.

Suddenly, the discovery of three little kids and two adults on the side of the road shifted our discussion. Now we faced a choice: should we help the family or leave them?

Our car was full, and we couldn't fit everyone in it. Still, could we leave them to weather the snowstorm stranded and alone without help? Back and forth our conversation went over what we should do. The discussion turned heated. My buddy Brian became angry. He wanted us to keep driving, so we wouldn't miss our midterms. He blamed the family for putting us in this predicament and tried to distance himself from the situation. "Who are these people?" he raged. "What kind of people would let their kids out there like that?"

Matt, a chubby sophomore, was the first to speak up and offer his seat. He volunteered to stay behind and wait for help. Then John, a sophomore wrestler, said they could have his seat, too. Conscience compounded, and everyone—except for Brian—willingly gave their seats in the car to the family.

Luckily, we could fit everyone into our car, leaving only two of my friends behind. It was a tight squeeze and a long drive to the next gas station, but we made it, and our two friends came in safely the next day. In the end, everything turned out fine. It also didn't hurt that the family we rescued was related to the dean, who postponed our exams.

The real story of this encounter wasn't that a family of five was rescued by a bunch of college boys. The real story is what caused Brian to act the way he did. Why was he the only one who refused to give up his seat? What did the rest of us value differently than Brian that prompted us to offer our places to the family?

First, Brian was attached to passing his midterm exams. It became the only thing he cared about. Not even the family with three children stranded on the road in a snowstorm could sway him. He allowed his fear over missing his exams and ignorance about the family and their situation overtake him and his ability to feel compassion for their plight. His fear and ignorance and his attachment to his personal needs overshadowed his compassion for others. Brian chose a survival-of-the-fittest mentality. His need to take his midterm exams and protect his welfare above all others was his only focus.

Second, for the rest of us, when we came upon the stranded family, it pushed against our basic instincts and emotions of compassion. Sandra Sucher, professor of management practice, and Nien-Hě Hsieh, associate professor of business administration at Harvard Business School, say in their paper "A Framework for Ethical Reasoning" that when we face moral judgments, we use our instincts and emotions to make an instantaneous decision. Rational analysis, they say, comes second.[1]

Instantly, five of us made a decision based on a shared value, but how could we all tap into the same value? Where did that compassion come from? We can't point to a shared religion because each of us had wildly different

---

1 Sandra Sucher and Nien-Hě Hsieh, "A Framework for Ethical Reasoning," *Harvard Business School*, 2011.

backgrounds. Two grew up Catholic, one Atheist, one Muslim, one Jewish, and myself, Hindu. We also came from diverse socioeconomic classes, families, and upbringings. Some of our parents were married while others were divorced.

Despite all these differences, we still united around shared values that prompted similar actions. According to the Dalai Lama, each of us is born with innate core values like compassion. It doesn't matter what socioeconomic level, religion, or personal situation you were born into, grow up in, or experience. Thus, compassion isn't a learned value but one waiting to be embraced.

"One of my fundamental beliefs is that not only do we inherently possess this potential or basis for compassion, but also the basic or fundamental nature is gentleness. Not only human beings but all sentient beings have gentleness as their fundamental nature," says the Dalai Lama.[2]

Recent studies support the Dalai Lama's beliefs. In his book *Just Babies: The Origins of Good and Evil*, Yale psychologist Paul Bloom says we're born with empathy and compassion; with the capacity to judge others and their actions; and with a basic understanding of justice and

---

2   The Dalai Lama, *Healing Anger: The Power of Patience from a Buddhist Perspective* (Snow Lion, 1997), 4.

fairness.[3] Other studies and research on infants and toddlers, by researchers such as Karen Wynn, professor of psychology and cognitive science at Yale University, have reached similar conclusions: that we're born with an ability to understand right from wrong, an instinct to drift toward the good versus the bad, and an understanding of sharing.[4]

## OUR INFLUENCES

I started my career honorably and with good intentions. I had strongly held values such as compassion, honesty, and respect. And just as I willingly gave up my seat in the car during the snowstorm, I also looked for ways to act compassionately and with respect in the workplace and toward my colleagues in the beginning.

I remember when I turned nineteen and I joined Ford Motor Company as a summer intern. I would walk the plant floor for hours monitoring assembly line machinery. I worked with men twice my age who made sure I remembered there was a divide between white- and blue-collar workers. They didn't accept me and I knew it. Gino, the most senior guy on the floor, was outright hostile to me. No matter what I said, he didn't believe that I was there

3    Paul Bloom, *Just Babies: The Origins of Good and Evil* (Crown, 2013).

4    Abigail Tucker, "Are Babies Born Good?" *Smithsonian Magazine*, January 2013, accessed February 10, 2016 (http://www.smithsonianmag.com/science-nature/are-babies-born-good-165443013/?no-ist=&page=2).

to learn. He told me to go back to school and that I was just like the rest of the management team.

Instinctually, I knew nothing I said would get through to him, so I turned to the universal language of food. Every day, I brought him Indian food, such as samosas and curry dishes that my mother made the night before. Gino was Italian, so I figured he would appreciate delicious home-cooked food.

Every day, I would ask him what he thought of my mother's cooking, and he would just shrug and look at me with anger.

On the seventh day, I asked him once again what he thought.

Instead of answering my question, he said something else.

"My son is dying from cancer," he said. There was no anger this time in his words, only sadness.

From that day on, he shared more about his life with me, and I told him about mine. We bonded on everything from watching our favorite sports teams together to playing cards during breaks. Soon I was going to barbecues with Gino and the rest of the men on the line.

I had connected on a human level with them because I used compassion, respect, and other core values that they responded to in kind. I treated my new friends with dignity and humanity. In turn, they treated me as an equal.

Many business leaders start their professional careers by acting on their values, but what happens that causes those values to sometimes fade? When I spoke with Professor Sucher of Harvard Business School, she explained, "The fact we're born with a certain kind of morality is true, but that morality and our values become shaped over time. It's in the shaping that things can either go well or not so well."[5]

This shaping that Professor Sucher refers to is the many outside factors influencing us from the moment we come into this world to our present day. Factors such as society, culture, media, our families, how we were raised, religion, friends, and our business environment all influence us, often without our realizing it.

This is what happened to me and is what's happening to millions of people.

I was born with innate values like everyone else, and my parents instilled even more values that complemented who I was at the core. My compassionate mother raised

5   Sandra Sucher, interview by author, September 17, 2015.

three children while working two retail jobs, while my loving father worked full time during the day as an engineer and at night as a professor of engineering at a nearby college. They came to the United States from India with very little in the way of money or material possessions. They came seeking new opportunities for themselves and their children.

I learned quickly from them the values of hard work, honesty, loyalty, compassion, and respect. They practiced those values every day, and those are values that I still hold close to me today.

Unfortunately, my parents weren't the only ones who influenced me at a young age. I grew up in a low-middle-class environment and a racially segregated neighborhood outside of Detroit. I was regularly bullied and frequently found myself in fights. I remember being teased many times for the color of my skin. Racial discrimination was an outlet for so many people struggling in our town, as the US automotive industry was beginning to lose its share of the market to global competition.

It wasn't a great environment to live in, and I knew I had to get out. But how?

On my way back from school every day, I would "escape"

by gazing at the billboards that hung over vacant buildings and empty lots. They would showcase famous models advertising various products, places, and things. From luxury car promotions to paradise cruises to high fashion advertisements, I began to consume the images. I watched shows such as *Lifestyles of the Rich and Famous* that profiled well-known celebrities, their lavish homes, and cars. I found comfort in these daydreams, and soon, they began to formulate my cultural expectations.

Pro athletes and celebrities became my heroes growing up. Fancy cars and clothes became my aspirations. This was what society valued—these people and material possessions. If that was society's definition of success and happiness, then it would be mine, too.

I grabbed on to these cultural hinges and societal strings that I thought could pull me out of my hard environment and achieve success.

The Dalai Lama says the purpose of life is to be happy.

*From the moment of birth, every human being wants happiness and does not want suffering. Neither social conditioning nor education nor ideology affects this. From the very core of our being, we simply desire contentment. I don't know whether the universe, with its countless galaxies, stars and planets, has a deeper meaning or not, but at the very least, it is clear that we humans who live on this earth face the task of making a happy life for ourselves. Therefore, it is important to discover what will bring about the greatest degree of happiness.*[6]

I thought I knew what would make me happy. My pursuit of a giant salary, big home, fancy job title, luxury car, and designer clothes—the things I thought I needed to free me from the environment I grew up in—overpowered me. But I didn't know it at the time. I believed I was being true to myself, that I was pursuing what would bring me happiness.

Unfortunately, these societal strings and cultural hinges clouded my core values. I didn't act from compassion, respect, honesty, or loyalty. Instead, my actions were driven by my desires to attain what I thought would make me happy or would help me to provide for my family.

At times, these desires influenced me to act in ways that, upon reflection later, were nothing short of shallow. My attachment to attaining certain images and my beliefs about what was happiness and who I was supposed to

---

6   The Dalai Lama, "Compassion and the Individual," accessed September 2, 2015 (http://www.dalailama.com/messages/compassion).

be gave me a false sense of who I really was and what I really wanted out of life.

For so long, I thought my happiness, or my purpose in life, was to attain these contrived attachments and material possessions. I flew up Maslow's hierarchy of needs, but once I reached a certain level, I found myself asking, "Now what?" Attaining my pleasures and passions only took me so far. Instead of being satisfied, content, and happy, I was floundering without any purpose.

"Our attitudes about money are more important than the amount we make,"[7] writes Howard C. Cutler, a psychiatrist and coauthor of numerous books with His Holiness the Dalai Lama. "As always, in our pursuit of happiness, our inner resources assume a greater role than our material resources."[8]

Now, to be clear, I'm a pure capitalist and believe in making money for myself and the greater good. I believe that it's OK to want and to enjoy a nice meal, sporting event, or concert. It's OK to want to drive a nice car and to live in a beautiful home. It's OK for us to have these aspirational pleasures and experiences. In fact, everyone should have the ability to achieve this if they want.

7   His Holiness the Dalai Lama and Howard C. Cutler, *The Art of Happiness at Work* (New York: Riverhead Books, 2003), 63.

8   Ibid.

However, these aspirations must be grounded on a purpose. Billboards must come with boundaries, and we need to remind ourselves of that. These desires potentially inspire all of us to create new products, services, and increase overall trade. All of this is essential in raising the human condition. We owe it to ourselves to provide equal and fair opportunities to one another. Capitalism can be that catalyst to elevate each of us in our lives and society as a whole.

But when we pursue pleasures, passions, and possessions at the cost of being true to ourselves, to the people around us, and to our own humanity, then our life spins off course. That is why *knowing* and *acting* on our core values, using our moral fiber, is needed to keep us from falling victim to the trappings of excessive greed and self-deception.

## CREATING TOXIC ENVIRONMENTS

The Buddha said, "You only lose what you cling to."[9]

Although I may have started my career looking for ways to act on my values, my fear of losing all I had attained—the money, the position, the title, the nice home, my security, and being able to provide for my daughter—drove me

---

9   ThinkExist, accessed August 24, 2016 (http://thinkexist.com/quotation/
    you-only-lose-what-you-cling-to/366035.html).

into a vicious cycle. I became conditioned to wanting and having these things in my life. I was strongly attached to those desires.

When we have a strong attachment to something, we want it; we're greedy for it. But if we can't get what we want, then we become angry. We act like a child who wants ice cream but whose mother says no. We then lash out in frustration and ignorance, pointing fingers at people who have what we desire. "Why is David getting paid more than me?" we'll say. Or, "Why is Jen being treated better than me?"

"As human beings we have good qualities as well as bad ones. Now anger, attachment, jealousy, hatred, are the bad side; these are the real enemy...the true troublemaker is inside," says the Dalai Lama.[10]

Buddhists believe three poisons—greed, hatred, and delusion (as I refer to as greed, anger and ignorance)—live inside each of us as unwholesome roots that cause our greatest suffering.[11] They believe we can trace all the negative thoughts and emotions we experience to these roots. When the poisons take hold and compound, they negatively affect our thoughts, emotions, and actions, causing us to lash out.

10  Mary Craig, ed., *The Pocket Dalai Lama* (Boston: Shambhala, 2002), 11,

11  Sunyata Buddhist Center, "Transforming the Three Poisons: Greed, Hatred, and Delusion," accessed March 16, 2016 (http://www.sunyatacentre.org/the-three-poisons/).

Learning this was an ah-ha moment for me.

My attachment to provide for my family and my desire to attain the material possessions that I believed would bring happiness to my life actually caused anger, greed, and ignorance to fester inside of me.

I realized that over the course of my career, I had grown infected with these poisons of anger, greed, and ignorance; so, too, have countless men and women in the corporate world. It was these emotions that pulled me away from my values and caused me to deceive myself.

In business, these three poisons run rampant through organizations. Of course, other poisons exist as well such as lust, pride, conceit, arrogance, jealousy, desire, insecurity, closed-mindedness, and fear, which also cause us to act in unhealthy, destructive, and damaging ways. For the purposes of this book, I'm focusing on anger, greed, and ignorance because I believe these are the three most critical in the creation of toxic environments.

When we act from these poisons, we begin to cripple our belief systems. Our attachment to things such as material possessions, providing for our families (at all costs), and other self-interests overpowers us, and we begin to scrape away our consciousness as individuals, organizations, and societies. This shreds our moral fiber. When we lose our moral fiber, we lose our ability to stay true to our values and ourselves in challenging and potentially compromising situations.

What many of us don't realize is that when we act on the poisons of anger, greed, and ignorance, we not only harm ourselves, but we also contribute to the toxic environments permeating our work cultures. The poisons are like a swarm of locusts that overtake our minds, slowly chipping away at our values.

Similarly, our minds act the same way. When one emotion, such as greed, enters, it's easier for us to control it. However, when the ill emotion flares, it attracts other negative thoughts and often breeds the other poisons. Once anger, greed, and ignorance have taken root, their friends such as fear, pride, jealousy, insecurity, and many more come to play. And just as swarms of locusts are difficult to eradicate, so, too, are the swarms of damaging emotions that infect and influence everyone in the environment.

We see these toxic behaviors play out in certain businesses, where some corporate cultures value quarterly earnings and shortcuts over long-term company growth. In fact, I believe profit-*only*-driven cultures are more likely to experience a greater degree of these poisons. In these environments, people become so keen on profits that they lose sight of how they attain them; rather than acting from their core values, people instead let anger, greed, and ignorance flare.

Another area where we see these poisons drip and contaminate our offices is on the corporate ladder. As we look at organizations, there are only a certain number of leadership positions available. As a result, competition to achieve these roles increases, creating greater opportunity for people to act from anger, greed, or ignorance in an attempt to achieve the prime position. Ultimately, this leads many people to compromise their core values, which then feeds into and creates toxic environments.

"The toxic work environment is one where people at the bottom are experiencing corrosive pressures, and these corrosive pressures are draining them and making them want to leave," explains Nancy Rothbard, management professor at Wharton Business School.[12]

## THE ENDLESS OFFER

Of the poisons I was afflicted with, greed drove me the hardest. It all began when I received a telephone call from

12  Wharton School of the University of Pennsylvania, "Is Your Workplace Tough—or Is It Toxic?," accessed September 12, 2015 (http://knowledge.wharton.upenn.edu/article/is-your-workplace-tough-or-is-it-toxic/).

Tamara in Human Resources early in my career. Standing in my one-bedroom apartment with white bare walls and a bed with no headboard, I listened as Tamara told me the team had loved me and they wanted to make me an offer.

Suddenly, my mind filled with anxiety. How much money would I make? What was my title? Would they cover the costs of my MBA, and if not, how would I pay for my loans? And then I heard her glorious words tell me they were offering me a six-figure salary, signing bonus, relocation stipend, *and* they would cover my education expenses.

My life was about to change. I was about to go from making about $30,000 a year to sitting in the six-figure club. *Finally*, I thought, *my life is going in the right direction.* I felt my humble environment crumble. *About time*, my ego roared to life.

This was when my desires took ahold of me. I didn't know it then, but ironically, my ticket to the six-figure club would see me earning less than my entry-level engineer's salary. Shortly after I joined Tamara's company, I went on a spending spree taking out loans to purchase a new home, car, furniture, and vacations.

I enjoyed myself and indulged in everything. I thought I deserved it. I paid my dues as a starving engineer, who had made almost nothing, and now it was my turn to get the rewards. My leftover pizza days were done; I was onto shrimp cocktail. I couldn't start my new job without a nice car or a beautiful home. I had to wear the finest brands. It was essential that I look the part of a six-figure club member. I was now swimming with sharks, and if I was perceived the wrong way by them, I could lose everything.

More opportunities, money, and stock options came to me early in my career. I relished these rewards, but the thought of losing it all began to hover over me. I became gripped by the fear of loss. Like many in management positions, I was forced to spend more time protecting my role in the company than searching for new, creative, and innovative ways to grow the business. Like many around me, I became risk averse and fixated on my next stock grant to pay for the new debt racked up that month.

My career and lifestyle began to own me. I felt crippled, owing more than what I made. I inadvertently slapped golden handcuffs around my wrists as I lived tomorrow's debt today. I had to keep this job, I remember thinking. I didn't see a way out of the lifestyle I had created for myself and my family. So I did what I had to do. I climbed the corporate ladder by focusing only on financial profits while embracing the corporate politics. I traveled frequently and worked long hours during the week and over the weekend.

It was all in the name of making more money, so that I could provide for my daughter and family. It was all in the name of my self-interests and attachments to what I thought was the source of my happiness.

## THE HATCHET BOY

Ignorance was another poison that challenged my core values. It was all around me. In one instance, I was promoted to lead a global business relationship with many resources worldwide. In taking this role, leadership made the obvious asks of me. They expected me to increase profit, revenue, and share while reducing costs. However, an interesting ask came to me over drinks one evening. One of my leaders, Jim, wanted me to manage out Damian who was on my team. I was told he wasn't delivering and was a difficult employee to work with.

I felt an obligation to Jim. As a leader, he helped make this career opportunity a reality for me. However, I didn't know Damian, his ability, skills, and personality, or how he would perform on my team. I was stuck. Do I follow the chain of command and push him out as I was asked to do, or do I push back on my leadership?

I wanted this position badly, and I didn't want to jeopardize it, so I rationalized what Jim asked of me. I invited ignorance and slowly started to form opinions about Damian, casting judgments about his work ethic, quality of product, and ability to work collaboratively on our team—except I never met him. When we finally did cross paths, he seemed very nice. My conscience told me not to remove him until I had a chance to work with and evaluate him.

So I asked Jim if he was fine with me testing things out with Damian. I thought maybe we could turn things around. But Jim quickly snapped at me, much to my surprise, and said no, he wanted Damian out immediately. Jim's quick, anger-laced response had me questioning whether I was appointed to this role simply to be the hatchet boy for Damian and potentially others who landed on Jim's hit list.

A week later, Jim gave me a stock bonus incentive and told me he saw a lot of good things happening in my future. That was the moment when I realized I wasn't being asked to get rid of my employee; I was being told to do so.

I wondered if I should go to Human Resources (HR) to discuss my dilemma. Would HR really help? Would I face retaliation? My career was at stake, but I didn't know what to do.

After some time, I decided to meet with HR. However, it

was more to learn about the options Damian could have. They shared with me that we could get him on a sixty-day performance management program to see how he performed before making any decision.

As Damian's new manager, I owed it to him and the company to ensure he was treated with respect throughout this process. At the same time, I had to be sure that he wasn't performing or achieving his deliverables as Jim stated.

I needed time to assess his work before letting Jim sway me with his toxic behavior. I didn't want ignorance to prevail. I went back to Jim to share that I was working with HR on a sixty-day performance plan. Jim was furious because he wanted Damian out immediately. However, he couldn't argue with the HR policy. More importantly, he couldn't cast blame or take it out on me.

After a great deal of research, I learned that it wasn't about Damian's inability to perform; rather, Jim had a personal grievance with him. I was tasked with terminating Damian because of a personal argument the two had gotten into a few years prior. Apparently, Jim was unintentionally embarrassed in front of a large audience, and this was his payback. More importantly, my assessment of Damian's performance after a few weeks was solid. He was doing a good job. Nevertheless, I also knew how the game was played. If Jim wanted someone out, I would be hard-pressed to stop him.

Unfortunately, many leaders like Jim abuse their power and influence to further their own personal agendas with their staff (e.g., nepotism, approving personal expenses, etc.). They believe their title is a badge and license to cause harm and foul for their own personal gain.

It would appear the party line "It's not personal; it's just business" is a lie.

It's *always* personal.

Especially when a manager masks his or her own malice in terminating an employee.

Regardless, saying, "It's not personal; it's just business," is a cowardly way of deflecting. If it was a business layoff and/or cost-cutting initiative, it's still personal because the receiving end of any cut or layoff is a human being.

"When people say, 'it's just business,' that's a way of numbing or distancing themselves," explains Mary Gentile, director of Giving Voice to Values and professor of practice at the University of Virginia Darden School of Business. "Even when it's a small action, that line is a mechanism that allows us to find ways to live with ourselves when we know we're making choices we're uncomfortable making."[13]

In the end, Damian left the company on his own. He was extremely hurt and chose not to be in this toxic environment any longer. Granted, he could have pleaded for a new role within the company or battled the sixty-day grind of the performance plan.

However, Damian knew the odds were stacked against him, and he would rather spend his energy finding the right home to flourish. If Damian remained at the company, I imagine he knew on some level that Jim's anger and ignorance would hover over his career, reducing any chances for him to survive or succeed. It was too bad how things ended. The company lost a great person and dedicated employee in Damian.

For me, the entire experience was difficult, even emotionally draining. From the moment that Jim asked me to let Damian go, to my talks with HR, to Damian's subsequent departure, I felt sick to my stomach and couldn't sleep for weeks. My values were being tugged, and my conscience was killing me over the situation. Was my happiness at the cost of another's well-being? How could I take on Jim, who was above me and could arguably control my future and

---

13 Mary Gentile, interview by author, September 10, 2015.

career? Did I have the courage to stand for what I believed was wrong? I knew in my gut and heart that Jim's actions weren't right, but what power did I have? Was it better for me to silence my inner voice? All these thoughts raced through my head as I felt caught in the middle.

I wish this wasn't true, but what happened to Damian happens every day in corporate environments. Anger, greed, and ignorance often prevail. In the moment, those emotions may feel pleasurable to us. In fact, we may even take joy in bathing in these seductive emotions as they can give us a false sense of fairness, happiness, and success.

But at what cost are we willing to tolerate this toxic behavior? What is the true cost to ourselves, lives, family, colleagues, and companies when anger, greed, and ignorance take ahold of us?

## MINDLESSLY WANDERING

It's nearly impossible to say whether more toxic environments exist in the workplace today than, say, fifty years ago. Mary Gentile, from the Darden School of Business, says the world we live in today may feel more toxic because of the speed, scope, range, and depth of communication available to us.[14]

---

14  Ibid.

Regardless of whether we're contending with more toxic environments, the reality is they exist. For thousands, more likely millions of us, we encounter them on a daily basis. These environments shape and influence our values and the way we act. When we watch leaders act from anger, greed, and ignorance, and we see them attain the wealth, titles, positions, and possessions we desire, we learn (often unconsciously) to believe that's the only path to success. In turn, we mimic those behaviors that have been directed toward us. Unfortunately, this drives us further away from our values and swings us to anger, greed, and ignorance, which only fuels profound feelings of unhappiness.

Essentially, we become caged, individually and organizationally, in this perpetual cycle where the people around us act from anger, greed, and ignorance, which influences us to do the same. In the end, all we've done is contribute to toxic environments. Our colleagues then become influenced by these behaviors and react the same way as a learned and conditioned behavior. This was the vicious pattern that took ahold of me and many of my colleagues.

Buddhists would call this pattern samsara, which is a continual repetitive cycle of mindless wandering between birth and death that arises from ordinary beings' grasping and fixating on a self and experiences.[15] The nineteenth-century Tibetan Lama Patrul Rinpoche explains the cyclic nature of samsara as follows: "The term samsara, the wheel or round of existence, is used here to mean going around and around from one place to another in a circle, like a potter's wheel, or the wheel of a water mill. When a fly is trapped in a closed jar, no matter where it flies, it cannot get out."[16]

Too many of us live in our own jars fluttering with no purpose—meaningless. We can only see what is immediately in front or behind us, not caring where the next stop light or road goes or comes from. We all have seen too many people wander in their careers and lives with no true intent. That was me.

Their compass is missing, or as Harvard Business School professor and former Medtronic chief executive officer (CEO) and author Bill George says in his book *True North*, "True North is the internal compass that guides you successfully through life ...When you follow your internal compass, your leadership will be authentic, and people will naturally want to associate with you."[17] He goes on

---

15  Georgetown University, Berkeley Center for Religion, Peace & World Affairs, "Samsara (Hinduism)," accessed February 28, 2016 (http://berkleycenter.georgetown.edu/essays/samsara-hinduism).

16  Patrul Rinpoche, *The Words of My Perfect Teacher*, trans. Padmakara Translation Group (Walnut Creek, CA: Altamira, 1998), 61–62.

17  Bill George, *Discover Your True North* (Hoboken, NJ: Wiley, 2015), xxiii.

to say, "Discovering your True North takes a lifetime of commitment and learning. Each day, as you are tested in the world, you yearn to look at yourself in the mirror and respect the person you see and the life you have chosen to lead."[18]

I call people missing their internal compass six-figure surfers, looking for the next big wave. Most call themselves opportunists, but they're grazing. They take in what they need to sustain their current lifestyle in their own jar, never thinking or caring how they may have treated people along the way. They contribute to the toxic environment, often without realizing it. All that matters to them is that they meet their immediate wants, pleasures, and desires.

ฝ   ฝ   ฝ

Are the poisons the only reason toxic environments exist? No, other factors exist in organizations that may also trigger and contribute to toxic environments. For example, how a company is structured, its processes, and its incentive packages can and do play a role. For this book, however, I'm focusing on the individual and what we can do in our lives to drive a better work environment. Having worked with many HR consultants for years in the areas of leadership and development, change management,

---

18  Ibid.

organizational structure, and performance management, I see many opportunities for companies to tackle this problem.

However, we cannot wait for our companies to enact this change. The greatest gain for us is at the individual level.

As the Dalai Lama says, "We will never solve our problems simply by instituting new laws and regulations. Ultimately, the source of our problems lies at the level of the individual. If people lack moral values and integrity, no system of laws and regulations will be adequate. So long as people give priority to material values, then injustice, inequity, intolerance, and greed—all the outward manifestation of neglect of inner values—will persist."[19]

We do, however, have control over our lives and the decisions we make, and we have the power to choose to act from our core values.

For many years, I worked in toxic environments—even contributing to some of them. My intentions were always good—I wanted to provide for my family. However, my approach was misguided, and I sometimes began to lose myself in those environments.

---

19  The Dalai Lama, *Beyond Religion: Ethics for a Whole World* (New York: Houghton Mifflin Harcourt, 2011), xii-xiii.

My life turned into a spinning wheel of activity, and I lost the essence of what I was working for, and why I was taking certain actions. I never stepped back to look closely or to inquire deeply about the type of businessperson I wanted to be in the corporate world. I never looked closely to find my true purpose and calling in business or in life.

It wasn't until after I met the Dalia Lama that I understood that I needed a cure to the toxins of anger, greed, and ignorance that consumed me. It's a cure that many of us in the corporate world so desperately need. That remedy is learning how to reawaken our core values, such as compassion, teamwork, and wisdom, and then acting on them.

But if we want to reawaken these core values and act on them, we first need to recognize a toxic environment and what toxic behaviors look like. In the next chapter, I'll walk you through the four most prevalent toxic behaviors that you're likely to see in the corporate world. When you can spot these behaviors, you'll recognize that you're working in a toxic environment.

CHAPTER 3

# CORPORATE SUFFERING

## THE FOUR DISEASES

———

DUKKHA *DEF.* SUFFERING,
UNSATISFACTORINESS, STRESS

Deception. Detraction. Discrimination. Doubt.

These are the four behavioral diseases that manifest in the office when people act from the three poisons of anger, greed, and ignorance. These diseases often overlap, and it isn't uncommon for someone to exhibit multiple behaviors or for one behavior to incite another. I define these four behavioral diseases as follows:

**Deception:** The act of deceiving; making someone believe something that is not true.

**Detraction:** The act of disparaging; belittling the reputation or worth of a person.

**Discrimination:** The practice of unfairly treating a person or group of people.

**Doubt:** A feeling of uncertainty or lack of conviction.

Whether it's one behavior or a combination that manifests, one thing is certain: mayhem and destruction follow in the wake, leading to the creation of toxic work environments. "These kinds of behaviors and environments lead to high stress and low morale," says Mary Gentile, from the Darden School of Business. "It also leads to less ethical behavior, because people feel like they have fewer choices, and they feel more constrained and fearful."[1]

More than likely, most people have no idea they're behaving this way. The majority of us don't act with ill intentions. We're acting without understanding or the awareness of what's really happening inside of us. The poisons of anger, greed, and ignorance are like termites living inside the walls of our homes. They survive for years without our knowing, without our realizing that our homes are slowly rotting from the inside out. That's what the poisons and the behavioral diseases inflict on us and our organizations.

---

1    Gentile, interview.

We may also use deception, detraction, discrimination, and doubt because we're mimicking our environments and the people we've observed, especially our leaders. Again, most of us do this unconsciously without stopping to ask if our behaviors match our values and the people we want to be.

How do these behavioral diseases manifest at the office? In the following pages, you'll read stories and examples of people behaving with deception, detraction, discrimination, and doubt. Hopefully, these stories will help you to see your work environment more clearly, how you're being treated, and perhaps how you're acting.

One important thing to note is that many of us who live in these toxic states for some time may begin to rationalize our behaviors. We will repeat the patterned behavior without any clear understanding of the harm it's causing us or how it's contributing to the toxic environments we work in.

The first step to changing is to become aware of its existence within and around you. As former Enron vice-president Sherron Watkins (internal whistle-blower) says, "If a frog is thrown in a pot of boiling water, it will jump out and save itself. If a frog is in a pot of cool water that is slowly heated, he'll stay in the pot until he boils to death."[2]

## BEHAVIORAL DISEASE: DECEPTION

*"A lack of transparency results in distrust and a deep sense of insecurity."*

— HIS HOLINESS THE DALAI LAMA[3]

Deception: The act of deceiving; making someone believe something that is not true.

Companies use what's called field stage events to bring people together to share important information and to galvanize the workforce toward the upcoming quarter. One year, I attended a field event that brought about a thousand of us together. Sitting in the fourth row, I craned my head to watch and listen as leaders paraded on stage to tell us about all the happenings at the company and what we could expect for the next quarter. Two hours into the event, the man sitting in front of me, Antonio, stood and walked to the stage.

2   Dick Carozza, "Interview with Sherron Watkins: Constant Warning," *Fraud Magazine*, January/February 2007 (http://www.fraud-magazine.com/article.aspx?id=583).

3   "The Best Dalai Lama Quotes," accessed May 11, 2016 (http://www.bestdalailamaquotes.com/quotes/a-lack-of-transparency-results-in-distrust-and-a-deep-sense-of-insecurity/).

This was a charismatic leader who charmed everyone. He ran the Asia division and worked closely with the CEO. In his talk, he stressed the importance of education, how we needed to help children, how it was critical to get technology into emerging markets, and how important it was to establish our presence in these places. I was enamored with his compelling storytelling and engagement with the audience.

As he closed his presentation, he invited anyone who wanted to join his team to reach out to him directly. Such an open invitation is practically unheard of in this company, but he said he was informal, casual, and extremely open.

He returned to his seat, and I thought this was my opportunity. I politely tapped him on the shoulder. Antonio turned and smiled as I told him what an amazing presentation that was and that I wanted to make a difference. He shook my hand and told me to e-mail him.

I left the gathering feeling great and having made a strong business connection. Following the event, I e-mailed Antonio. I was interested in learning more about how I could help him in his goals. After several attempts of getting in touch with him, I finally heard from his assistant who scheduled a meeting between us.

On the day of our meeting, I walked into his office, and everything I thought I had known about him, based on the image he presented on stage, imploded. His office was like the Taj Mahal. I waited for about twenty minutes looking around in awe over the size, magnitude, and decor. Some leaders keep positive affirmations and inspirational pictures around their offices, but this one was littered with different awards and photos of self-ego and people Antonio had conducted business with such as heads of state and prime ministers.

When I finally met with him, I told him I was impressed, but he brusquely brushed off my comments and wanted to know what the meeting was about. I quickly pivoted and explained that I wanted to see if there was any opportunity, either full or part time, on a project with his team. I even asked if I could volunteer part-time during my off hours in my current role.

He asked how long I'd been with the company and which executives I knew. Once he learned I was in my first year and not well connected, he said there wasn't much he could do for me. His response took me off-guard given his presentation and open invitation.

Many leaders leverage empathy to connect with employees. For example, they say they're open to having a conversation, but then they don't follow through. Like many, I was eager and ready to work hard, but Antonio's priorities sat in his treasured tomb.

This type of deception—when something is said one way in public and another way in private—is a form of hypocrisy. Sadly, it's a common behavior in the corporate world. People say one thing, such as they embrace teamwork, open communication, and trust, but then their behaviors contradict their words. Sometimes the hypocritical behavior is intentional and sometimes unintentional. Regardless, it erodes trust, which is fundamental in business, and we all need to be more aware of what's happening.

Every day, we see companies and people deceive others to get what they want. Deception can take many forms—from individuals masking résumés on LinkedIn to companies falsely advertising, to manipulative behavior. If you see any of these behaviors, it's often a sign that you're working in a deceptive environment.

Another example is one of my old colleagues, Sherri, who ran a worldwide marketing team. The first time I saw her walk into a room, I thought she was an amazing leader. She was great talking with people and seemed to solve every problem. Then I found out she was often the cause of the problems. She regularly pitted one leader against the other, manufactured a problem, and then she was ready to fix the situation.

Deceptive behaviors, such as the manipulation that Sherri caused, happen because people need to showcase their own value. Greed, one of the poisons, often drives this behavior, because people desperately want to succeed. Success to them is making more money and getting promoted. In many companies, climbing the ladder is expected. In those hallways, the mantra is "Manage up or manage out."

As Joe Gullo, business leader at Rambus, shared with me, "I don't think companies have become more toxic. They're just moving from an overt, explicit level of toxicity to one that's subtler but equally damaging. Early in my career, I had my car vandalized in the employee parking lot. Today, I have people practicing deceptive behavior like promising me things that they never follow through with."[4]

## BEHAVIORAL DISEASE: DETRACTION

*When another person makes you suffer, it is because he suffers deeply within himself, and his suffering is spilling over. He*

---

4   Joe Gullo, interview by author, September 28, 2015.

*does not need punishment; he needs help. That's the message*
*he is sending.*

— THICH NHAT HANH[5]

Detraction: The act of disparaging; belittling the reputation
or worth of a person.

Detraction is a toxic behavior prevalent in corporations
where the environment teems with a high level of aggres-
sion. In these environments, people use intimidation and
bullying tactics toward others. They manage through
fear, and they demonstrate a high level of cynicism and
self-serving behavior. It's an extremely hating environment where people belittle, gossip, slander, and put others
down in order to get ahead.

Three months into a new job, I was given the task to
drive a leadership and development program for global
field leaders in an emerging technology business. It was
potentially a $10-billion growing sector for the company.
I was handed a group of consultants to lead this effort
and a six-month time frame to execute. My manager,
Larry, had been with the company for about five years

---

5    "Best Thich Nhat Hanh Quotes," *Gaia*, June 24, 2015 (http://www.gaia.
     com/article/well-wishes-luminary-thich-nhat-hanh).

CORPORATE SUFFERING · 85

and he reported directly to the vice-president, who ran the product team for this business. Larry was a stocky, charismatic guy. He was intuitive, smart, and considered a strong internal facilitator within the company. He was known for strongly influencing people and getting them to do what he wanted.

He also had a quick temper, which he showed when things didn't go his way.

Little things would set him off, and you never knew what would spark his anger. He'd simply lose control of how to handle himself or the situation. Often, he overpromised to gain commitment on a project, and when he failed to deliver—which happened regularly—people chose to leave his team.

One day, we invited all the worldwide leaders, almost thirty people, to a conference. For three days, we discussed strategy and execution in these conference rooms, at team events, and over dinners and drinks. Leaders traded off giving their presentations and proposals as they sat at long tables organized in a U-shape. Executives from other businesses and leaders much senior than Larry were in the room. Larry gave his presentation of the highs and lows, and then he took every opportunity to throw punches at various regions in shameful ways as others gave presentations.

During one presentation, Larry wouldn't let the man finish his presentation, jumping in and slandering him at every opening. He made jokes and called him names. Simon was from South Korea, and Larry asked if he was working in North Korea versus South Korea. He belittled him personally and on his business performance in front of his peers. I was horrified by this behavior. The saddest part was that no one came to Simon's rescue. No one stopped Larry because intimidation set in and fear plastered the room.

On another day, it was my turn to get raked in front of people. Larry was a no-show for a meeting with the vice-president who ran a large business group and who worked closely with the CEO. At the last moment, Larry asked me to present on his behalf. I'm sure Larry thought he was going to get slaughtered because of our numbers, so he sent me instead to take the heat. I was only three months into this position, but I walked into the conference room and stood in front of about twelve leaders. Minutes into what was supposed to be a twenty-five-minute presentation, the vice-president stopped me and began precision questioning.

Unfortunately, this form of questioning can also be used negatively to intimidate people. I have seen it used too often to instill fear, rattle and rathole people on certain numbers and topics, and belittle them in front of their peers. Rather than being used to better understand or gain greater clarity it was used more often to expose a person and his or her mishaps. Instead of saying, "OK, you know what? It looks like you didn't really get this one. Let's figure out what happened, and we'll move to the next topic," many leaders use this to exploit and humiliate people for their own benefit.

At the end of my presentation, the vice-president lifted a copy of my presentation over his head and asked me in a demeaning tone, "What's the one thing I'll remember?" I started to walk him through key components of the presentation, but he halted me and screamed at me.

"No, one thing!"

"I don't know what you'll remember," I said.

"You'll never survive here," he curtly replied.

The vice-president used this behavior to instill fear and to bully me and many others. Once he demonstrated that this behavior was OK, others followed. Every time he asked a question, someone else would take a shot at me like it was some game.

At the end of the presentation, another executive

approached me, patted me on the back, and said I did a good job. Suddenly, others followed suit and offered me similar congratulations. This disturbed me. I started to notice a trend as I attended more meetings. Whenever a recent hire was in the room, this bullying and fear-based behavior was used. It was like being initiated into a fraternity and this was the hazing process all the new people had to endure to earn their stripes.

This one board room example demonstrates the numerous forms that detraction can take in the workplace. Both Larry and the vice-president were highly aggressive, intimidating bullies, who worked to instill fear in me and others in the room. This type of behavior is also self-serving. It shows everyone in the room who is in control.

People like Larry and the vice-president threaten people to fall in line. They surround themselves with yes-men, people who will validate their decisions and power. If anyone pushed back, their career was over. Many leaders talk and preach about wanting diversity of thought, pushback, and to be challenged, but few actually incorporate it. Instead, they invite deception to join their detractive behavior.

Also, detraction does not discriminate. I have seen many people use this across all cultures in various forms. For example, you don't have to be loud and from a Western culture to detract. I've witnessed many Asian cultures that silently detract and use gossip as the cultural norm to exploit an employee. In Europe and Latin America, I have seen many leaders leverage the "mob" mentality. For example, it's not your merit or what you say that defines you but rather, what everybody else says and how they say it about you that define your brand and reputation that is more important. In a matter of hours, I have seen careers fall because of fabricated stories published via social media in these markets.

Leaders treat people like this because they believe, or they're told, that fear is the best motivator of people. But this isn't a sustainable practice. Good, talented people leave environments plagued by detraction and laced with fear. Remember Simon from South Korea that Larry belittled in the meeting? Within three months of that incident, he went to a direct competitor and doubled his income all while stealing more share and revenue from Larry's business.

Besides being told that fear is a strong motivator, people also use it as a shield to protect themselves when they feel threatened. This often happens when a new employee joins the company that has attributes and strengths that we don't. Suddenly, we become afraid and insecure that they'll easily surpass or outshine us in the next performance review, so we arm ourselves with anger to push away the perceived danger. As His Holiness the Dalai Lama says in his book, *Healing Anger*, "Anger acts as a protector."

This fear and insecurity comes in as one thought and then multiplies, like locusts, compounding the mind with negativity. I've witnessed many careers end because of someone's fear of another employee. And the company is harmed as well when this happens. Individuals riddled with fear and insecurity press for competition—but the unhealthy kind, where someone is focused on beating and standing out from the pack, instead of working together to elevate themselves and the company to new heights. It isn't long before a company starts to hire and promote the people exhibiting the worst behaviors.

## BEHAVIORAL DISEASE: DISCRIMINATION

*It is not our differences that divide us. It is our inability to recognize, accept, and celebrate those differences.*

— AUDRE LORDE[6]

Discrimination: The practice of unfairly treating a person or group of people.

---

6    Audre Lorde, *Our Dead behind Us: Poems* (New York: Norton, 1994).

Discrimination comes in many forms. One form it takes is in cliquishness. This is an "insiders and outsiders" mentality rather than one of unification and teamwork within an organization. We're exposed to discrimination when we're children, and it carries through to the corporate world. If you think back to your high school experience, then you'll likely remember seeing discrimination in the hallways. People separated into different groups and different cliques based on extracurricular activities and popularity.

The same mentality and behavior exist in the corporate world. Although discrimination is extremely toxic, many view it as a key component to their success and ability to climb the proverbial ladder. Whom and when you associate with someone plays an integral role in whether you advance in your career. These relationships can also help you to navigate and influence key decision makers on the projects or initiatives you're driving within the organization.

I learned this quickly. When you become tight with a particular group of people who don't allow other folks, the act of discrimination occurs. On the outside, it may appear harmless, wholesome even, because you're trying to create strong alliances for yourself. You're aligning yourself with key people, which is a good thing. However, when those key people, or you, start pulling away from others and not accepting them, you're in essence practicing a form of discrimination. And it's easy for detraction to leak in as your group may verbally gossip or put people down.

Sometimes discrimination happens unknowingly, but unfortunately, many people knowingly discriminate against others in the office. There are a number of reasons why this happens. One, it's as simple as someone doesn't like the other person, so he or he may not want that person to join his or her team. Other times, it's a strategic move because associating with a specific person may hinder his or her career. Often, I've seen discrimination happen when a company's bottom line and margins are low for the year or the coming years. Tough margins foster toxic behaviors, especially discrimination, which is used as a form of survival. People don't want to be associated with someone who didn't hit his or her bottom line for the quarter or year; they want to be associated with the winners.

Another form of discrimination is favoritism. Favoritism, stems from the alliances formed, which is why people look to form them with key people while discriminating against others. Favoritism takes place through the top ranks of a company. I've watched as executives formed their crews who got everything they needed. This happens in every industry. When new leaders take over a company, at times, they'll wipe out the existing leadership team to bring in their own team. Unfortunately, they may transition their teams too quickly by making the wrong hiring and firing decisions, which leads to having the wrong people in certain roles.

Insincere communication is another form of discrimination. This comes back to haunt leaders and individuals and is a symptom of ignorance. Typically, the individual on the receiving end of an insincere communication remembers what was told or said to them. I've seen people who have said things and then, surprisingly, that individual was fired because the other person got promoted and he or she never forgot what happened or how he or she was treated. This action soils and stains the work environment with fear. It also causes people to cease saying what's on their mind and doing what's right for the business because they're afraid of the reaction from their leaders and colleagues.

For example, I shouldn't be afraid to express my opinion and business recommendations because my manager has a different viewpoint. Unfortunately, this happens and people hesitate in speaking. Often, they're unwilling to honestly express their opinions for fear their manager will hammer them with a form of insincere communication.

Insincere communication also comes in the form of bullying and aggressive behavior. One day, your manager will yell at you and the next he or she is your best friend. Those actions bleed throughout the organization and can remain for many years, taking a long time for it to leave the halls. When this behavior strikes, it causes people to walk on eggshells wondering if today will be a good or bad day. Like the other behaviors, this breeds fear within people who worry they'll be scolded.

In some companies, managers are taught to manage their people through fear. Thus, every act is designed to accomplish that directive. It's a way they hold people accountable. Unfortunately, this behavior can become normalized and people end up close minded and close hearted. The result is a work environment where people come for the sake of collecting their paychecks instead of working and doing the right things for the business and their teams. I have lived in these types of environments for many years, and it is sad to see so many leaders turn a blind eye and perpetuate this behavior.

## BEHAVIORAL DISEASE: DOUBT

*Your worst enemy cannot harm you as much as your unguarded thoughts.*

— BUDDHA[7]

Doubt: A feeling of uncertainty or lack of conviction.

Joseph Goldstein, author of *Mindfulness*, explains there are two usages for the word *doubt*. The first has to do with inquiry and investigation. Doubt of something—an idea, a person, a situation, or a fact—can motivate us to examine things more carefully. The Dalai Lama encourages us to always continue to ask the question "Why?" Doubt used in this way, to answer "why" questions is beneficial, because it encourages us to gain greater wisdom and knowledge. However, for doubt to play this role, it must be rooted in the intention of inquiry and investigation to ensure we're being true to ourselves.

The shadow part of doubt, which we often see in the corporate world, is when it causes a state of uncertainty, wavering, and indecision. This type of doubt fosters

---

7     Elisha Goldstein, "Just Remember: Thoughts Aren't Facts," *The Huffington Post*, July 17, 2013 (http://www.huffingtonpost.com/elisha-goldstein-phd/just-remember-thoughts-ar_b_3287836.html).

more doubt, which is bad in business. Having this type of doubt outside of inquiry and investigation causes serious problems. For example, a company trying to do due diligence on a merger and acquisition needs to ask the right questions but not get trapped in an endless question-and-answer session.

Is it normal for people to have some doubt about whether they've made the right decision? Yes. Is it normal for people to second-guess whether they should have put $50,000 toward a particular marketing campaign? Yes. Some doubt is common, but it becomes toxic when we continuously circle around those doubts without any conviction.

This leads to excessive consensus building and validation before making any decisions, which limits a company's agility to react to competitive threats or to address immediate market needs or customer wants. When this happens, bureaucracy takes over. People become afraid to make a decision, so they'll pass the decision to someone else or they'll prolong having to make the decision.

Their greed, ego, and self-preservation kicks in because they don't want accountability for making a decision that leads to a poor, disappointing, or disastrous outcome. If doubt causes leaders to delay making decisions or prolong the release of a new product, then doubt has become toxic because it's hindering growth and productivity of the organization.

Rick Wong, a former vice-president at Microsoft, has seen the damage doubt and fear of failure can do within an organization. In one instance, his team was competing with new product categories that would utterly change his company's business model.

"We had to change," says Wong, "because our old form of business wasn't going to survive. This sort of change requires hard decisions. Any time you move on to something new, it always means you have to leave the comfort of what you knew behind. But no one wanted to be the one to make that decision, because what if they failed?"[8]

Rick participated in many meetings where the primary goal was to decide whether to move forward in this new direction or to stay the course. They would follow the agenda until right before the meetings was about to end when a key decision maker would ask a question no one could answer. This unanswerable question became justification for not making a decision. This happened multiple times until finally, they realized they were behind the market and their product development.

8   Rick Wong, interview by author, September 29, 2015.

The decision should have been made sooner. "The same leaders, who asked the questions that prevented us from moving forward, were now pointing fingers and blaming others for being too slow and not moving faster. These people did everything they could to shed the decision-making responsibility," says Wong.

When a company stops growing as fast as it used to, doubt forms. In this instance, success is redefined from the macro-level (success of the company) to the micro-level (success of an individual). When you're not winning externally in the market, then it becomes who wins internally at the company. People jockey to claim the title as the smartest person in the room. It's a game of who can talk the good talk, whether they walk it or not.

The worst thing you can do is be wrong because that means you're not the smartest person in the room. People start pointing fingers at others as self-preservation kicks in. If they can delay making the big decisions, they can delay failing or looking as if they aren't the smartest person in the room. If they can show that they're smarter than the others in the room, then their odds of surviving cuts, layoffs, or restructuring improves.

Doubt also happens when we cannot tell the difference between wholesome and unwholesome thoughts. As

Goldstein explains, without this, we are unable to overcome the forces of greed, aversion, and delusion in the mind. Because we don't know what brings us happiness and what brings suffering, we remain stuck in taking wrong actions, which breed further doubt.[9]

ૐ   ૐ   ૐ

His Holiness the Dalai Lama told me we cause our own suffering. I believe it's in the foliage of our own deception, detraction, discrimination, and doubt where hues of anger, greed, and ignorance prevail, caging our minds with ill intent.

Blaming organizations is an easy path displacing accountability. Introspection is difficult as it calls on *us* to change, thus, requiring individual effort and discipline. Each of us has a responsibility to manage the poisons within ourselves, so we can contribute positively and productively at work.

When we familiarize and identify the root causes (anger, greed, and ignorance) of the toxic behaviors of deception, detraction, discrimination, and doubt, we can then become aware of them. Once we're aware of them, we can then manage them. These are the first steps required

9   Joseph Goldstein, *Mindfulness: A Practical Guide to Awakening* (Sounds True, 2013), 167.

to elevating ourselves and releasing ourselves from the poisons and the influence of the toxic environments we work in.

Once we know how to spot working in a toxic environment, the next step is to return to our core values. In the following chapter, I'll show you how to start that process.

# CHAPTER 4

# UNVEILING CORPORATE CONSCIOUSNESS

---

VINNANA *DEF.* CONSCIOUSNESS

"Your work environment is only toxic if you let it be toxic," says Rick Wong, former vice-president at Microsoft.[1] He's right. We all have choices in our lives. We can choose to mindlessly wander the path of samsara, allowing toxic environments and people to influence us. We can choose to act on the three poisons—anger, greed, and ignorance. Or we can choose to return to our values, act on them, and in turn, strengthen our moral fiber.

---

1   Wong, interview.

When we strengthen our moral fiber—through embracing our core values and then acting on them—we succeed in business by being true to ourselves, instead of compromising who we are. And as our moral fiber grows, we'll find those toxic environments and the behaviors of deception, detraction, discrimination, and doubt that once influenced us (and that we may also have contributed to) start to crumble.

Or, rather, we'll rise above them, even when challenging events and experiences occur. "My values give me the courage to help navigate compromising situations," says Joanne Harrell, Board of Regents at the University of Washington and former board director of REI. "Courage is a hard thing in business, perhaps the hardest thing of all."[2]

Brian Kieley, who enjoyed a long, successful career as a senior vice-president at VISA running the Global Customer Service Division, witnessed the power of knowing and acting on his values. Brian once managed a staff of more than fifteen hundred people scattered throughout the world in thirty locations and eighteen countries. Despite excellent performance reviews, bonuses, and feedback from the people around him, one day Brian was told the company decided to go in a different direction with his position. He was, to his surprise, no longer needed.

2    Joanne Harrell, interview by author, September 29, 2015.

Brian was given two options: he could take a severance package and leave immediately, or he could remain and run the team until his successor was found.

Brian chose to stay. "It was really difficult, especially emotionally," says Brian. "Everyone around me, including the person who told me I had to leave, said I'd done a great job. Yes, I could have taken the package and walked away immediately, but I didn't want to abandon my team. They trusted and respected me, and I wanted to do what was best for them and help lead them through this transition."[3]

In coming to his decision, Brian looked deep within himself to understand what he valued most, which was remaining loyal to his team. He stood by his values and stayed true to himself despite a challenging situation. His values of respect, loyalty, and compassion were values he chose to live his life by, even within the halls of the corporate world.

Brian's experience isn't unique. He and many others have enjoyed successful careers by many factors. They've moved through the ranks of major corporations to become executives and managed hundreds of people and numerous divisions. Even more astounding is they've achieved this material and career success by remaining

3    Brian Kieley, interview by author, September 17, 2015

true to themselves and without compromising their values despite the toxic environments they operated within. Time and again, they acted on their values. Brian and many others show us a world where it's possible to be successful in business while being true to ourselves, despite challenging circumstances and experiences.

If they can be successful and elevate themselves above these corrosive environments surrounding them, then so can each of us.

## REDISCOVER YOUR VALUES

The key to unlocking the golden handcuffs and to freeing ourselves from the mindless wandering of samsara is to build our moral fiber. I like to think of my moral fiber as representing the thread of consciousness inside of me that reminds me of my core values, the person I want to be, and my purpose in life. As our moral fiber strengthens, our ability to navigate and rise above any toxic situation or person increases and becomes easier.

Our moral fiber consists of two parts: knowing our values and then acting on them. This is how we strengthen it.

However, before we can act on our values, we first need a deep understanding of *what* we value. This step is about defining our core values, instead of having our values defined by others or suppressed by our environments. For me, I rediscovered my core values and gained greater clarity about who I am and who I want to be in the business world by developing a deeper self-awareness, practicing mindfulness, and developing a keen eye for introspection.

The dictionary definition of the word *value* says it's "a person's principles or standards of behavior; one's judgment of what is important in life." As I wrote in chapter 2, we're born with certain innate values such as compassion and the ability to know right from wrong. But outside factors such as our families, religion, environment, upbringing, media, and friends shape, layer, and mold our values.

Over time, our core values can potentially become buried under the influence of these outside factors. "What society rewards can be a powerful influence and that's why it matters whom we look up to. Who is being rewarded? Who is given airtime? Who makes the cover of the magazine?" says Nien-hê Hsieh, associate professor of business administration at Harvard Business School.[4] Unfortunately, these societal strings and social nuances can warp our core beliefs and give us a false sense of being true to ourselves.

---

4   Nien-hê Hsieh, interview by author, September 9, 2015.

The good news is that no matter how buried or faded our values, we haven't lost them. Those core values still exist within us. We just have to find them again and strengthen them.

So what are those core values? In her work on values, Mary Gentile, from the Darden School of Business, has discovered that when you ask most people what they value, it boils down to a widely shared list that includes honesty, respect, responsibility, fairness, and compassion.[5]

Gentile's findings appear in line with Jonathan Haidt's work on moral foundations. A leading researcher in the field of morality and emotions and professor at the New York University Stern School of Business, Haidt cocreated the moral foundations theory with other social psychologists. The theory proposes that several innate and universally available psychological systems are the foundations of "intuitive ethics." The five foundations include care, fairness, loyalty, authority, and sanctity.[6]

For me, the values that ring true to my core include honesty, compassion, loyalty, and respect. In many ways, universal values are like a common denominator, that over time we formulate and tailor for ourselves. If you

---

5   Mary Gentile, *Giving Voice to Values* (New Haven, CT: Yale University Press, 2010), 24.

6   Moral Foundations, accessed March 4, 2016 (http://www.moralfoundations.org/).

ask multiple people what they value, you'll likely hear variations. Figure 1 presents the diversity of values that a few business executives and leaders shared with me in a series of interviews.

When I spoke with Sandra Sucher, professor of management practice at Harvard Business School, we talked about the importance of values. She told me that "strong values provide a common framework for understanding the goals and aspirations of the company and the kind of organization it wants to be. Strong values provide guardrails around actions, helping organization members to self-monitor and helping groups to challenge each other when they are approaching an unsafe zone. Strong values aid in decision making and can create consistency in behavior over time to produce an organization with a distinct set of values and behaviors that it habitually uses to act on them."[7]

I urge you to consider writing down your own list of core values. You can use the ones I mentioned for myself and those of other business leaders in figure 1 as inspiration. Or another useful place to help you rediscover your core values is to look at your organization. Identify leaders you admire or even those you don't. Leaders set the tone and determine what the organization stands for. It's easy for a leader to say his or her company values transparency,

---

7    Sucher, interview.

# WHAT BUSINESS LEADERS VALUE

"Justice, Collaboration, Respect, Excellence, and Integrity."

LISA FELICE, PHD, ORGANIZATIONAL PSYCHOLOGIST AND CONSULTANT

"Transparency, Honesty, Fairness, Passion, and Empathy."

STEVE GUGGENHEIMER, CORPORATE VICE-PRESIDENT
AND CHIEF EVANGELIST AT MICROSOFT

"Rational Thought, Curiosity, Fairness, and Honesty."

JOE GULLO, BUSINESS LEADER AT RAMBUS

"Perseverance, Integrity, Courage, and Desire to Learn."

JOANNE HARRELL, BOARD OF REGENTS, UNIVERSITY OF
WASHINGTON & FORMER BOARD DIRECTOR OF REI

"Integrity, Respect, Kindness, Learning, and Hard Work."

LUCY HUR, SENIOR VICE-PRESIDENT, PARTNER RESOURCES, STARBUCKS

"Honesty, Respect, Inclusion, Transparency, Openness, and Compassion."

BRIAN KIELEY, FORMER SENIOR VICE-PRESIDENT
GLOBAL HEAD CLIENT SUPPORT SERVICES AT VISA

"Straightforward Communication, Creativity, Drive, and Accountability."

ROBIN O'CONNELL, EXECUTIVE VICE-PRESIDENT, UPHOLD INCORPORATED

"Respect, Love, Vulnerability, Action, Accountability, and Fun."

BRIAN ROSE, FOUNDER AND HOST OF LONDON REAL

"Integrity, Smarts, Communication, and Continuous Learning."

PATRICK SHANNON, PARTNER AT MERCER CONSULTING

"Selflessness, Patriotism, and Loyalty."

COLONEL KARL WALLI (RET.), PHD

"Respect, Humility, and Accountability."

RICK WONG, FORMER VP AT MICROSOFT AND
SALES LEADER AT HEWLETT-PACKARD

FIGURE 1

but if information is hoarded, meetings secretive, and employees largely kept in the dark on everything, transparency isn't a value. If this upsets you, then perhaps transparency is an important core value to you.

I've noticed the organizations with the healthiest cultures have strong, admirable leaders who walk the walk with their values. These men and women not only state what they value, but their actions also align with them. This of course influences the rest of the organization in a healthy, positive way. The five common values I've witnessed in organizations with outstanding leadership include the following:

## EMPATHY

In business, having empathy means listening, understanding, and caring about your colleagues and subordinates. It's the ability to really understand where someone is coming from, even if you disagree with his or her ideas and actions. Empathy is a crucial value that leads to building trust among team members, in turn creating a unified force. There is no ill will or malicious intent. Instead of people wondering if their teammate is going to throw them under the bus, there is acceptance and cooperation. This one value, when acted upon, creates a platform that can promote greater creativity of thought and innovation throughout the organization.

## COMPASSION

I've worked under many leaders throughout my career, and the ones I respected the most set aside their egos and listened with sincerity and humility. They displayed a vested interest in learning more about their employees and colleagues, and the compassion they showed toward them inspired and motivated them to be better employees and team members.

"I'm a big believer in practicing what you preach, or don't ask others to do what you're not willing to do yourself," says Steven Guggenheimer, corporate vice-president and chief evangelist at Microsoft. "You've got to be willing to get your hands dirty or do the work that you would ask others to do. It's not enough to have sympathy or just an idea of what people do. You actually have to have done it, so you know what it's like for them."[8]

As the Dalai Lama says, "Compassion reduces fear, boosts our confidence, and opens us to inner strength. By reducing distrust, it opens us to others and brings us a sense of connections with them and a sense of purpose and meaning in life."[9]

---

8    Steve Guggenheimer, interview by author, September 29, 2015.

9    The Dalai Lama, *Beyond Religion*, 45.

## HONESTY

"If you live your life honestly and truthfully, then you'll be open and transparent, which leads to trust. And trust leads to friendship,"[10] says the Dalai Lama. Honesty in our interactions with colleagues and associates is necessary to build a strong foundation of trust, which is a must in business. Achieving trust requires us to show vulnerability, authenticity, and integrity. This is about being honest and transparent with ourselves and others. Most of us distance ourselves from being vulnerable. We've been taught it provokes weakness, yet ironically, it's our greatest strength. Forgiving ourselves, and taking responsibility for our decisions and actions, lets us reset. At the same time, it showcases executive maturity that we have learned and grown from that experience.

## LOYALTY

In today's ultracompetitive business environment, loyalty is critical in driving agile decision making and forging lasting relationships with colleagues and customers. In business, we'll often see new leaders bring in their own team from previous positions and companies. That's because leaders need loyal people who will get the job done for them. Most often, loyalty comes over time

---

10   The Dalai Lama, Twitter posted December 2015, accessed March 30, 2016
     (https://twitter.com/dalailama/status/681421955531051008).

through trusted relationships with colleagues or customers. However, it can be earned quickly through indirect relationships and vouching for others. For example, one may hire an individual based on a recommendation of trusted coworker.

## RESPECT

Another key value in business is mutual respect that flows up and down the chain of command. How many times have you watched colleagues trip up their careers by going above their manager without informing them? Similarly, how many times have you seen managers never give air cover to their employees when it was needed? A leader cannot command or purchase deep admiration and respect from the people they work with or those who report to them; it's earned by demonstrating the core universal values that show their people they care, understand, and can help.

## THE GATEWAY: SELF-AWARENESS

Now that we have discussed some universal values, it's time to rediscover yours. One tool that was especially helpful to me was self-awareness. In fact, self-awareness is like a gateway because it's through this path that we begin to understand what motivates us to act in certain ways.

Being aware of our values is the first step in balancing the three poisons of anger, greed, and ignorance.

Like many leaders, my actions and decisions were motivated by my desire to attain certain levels of success in the corporate world. Unfortunately, I paid a heavy cost: being true to myself and my values. This level of honesty about ourselves is tough. Most of us avoid it. Unfortunately, for me, it took a great deal of both personal and professional hardship to force me to reflect on my initial intent, motivations, feelings, and thoughts, and whether I was the person I wanted to be.

Nien-hê Hsieh, an associate professor of business administration at Harvard Business School who researches ethics and business, shared with me that this avoidance of introspection is not uncommon. "I think a lot of times we aren't aware of what we're doing, or we don't think about what we're doing and why we're doing it, because we're afraid to dig deep and be honest with ourselves," he explains.[11] "But if we can confront that fear and explore why we do what we do and what we're trying to achieve, then we're likely to experience greater happiness and purpose in our lives."[12]

---

11  Hsieh, interview.

12  Ibid.

Although challenging, many leaders say the key to their success and ability to be true to themselves amid an often-toxic corporate world has come through self-awareness. "People who are self-aware will separate themselves rather than conform to people who make poor decisions, especially harmful or dangerous ones," explains Lisa Felice, PhD, organizational psychologist and consultant.[13] "But employees who lack self-awareness are at risk for conforming, which can negatively impact the organization and its culture over time."[14]

Self-awareness requires a calmness of mind in order to take an introspective view of how you've acted and who you want to be. But how many of us carve out a few minutes every day to let our minds relax and to reflect? I never used to. It felt impossible with my schedule built out from the moment I woke up to the time I went to bed.

In fact, my father used to say to me as a kid, "Shawn, at the end of the day and before you go to sleep, lie in bed and think for five minutes about what you accomplished for that day. Think about how you used your time."

I used to laugh and roll my eyes at that suggestion and never did it, but now I take at least five minutes to check

---

13   Lisa Felice, interview by author, October 13, 2015.

14   Ibid.

in and ask what I accomplished for the day. I'll reflect on what I wanted to get done and whether I was able to finish it. This isn't necessarily about checking off our to-do lists and seeing how many activities we achieved. It's more about identifying if we made a difference. It's about asking ourselves how we did overall, like did our actions seek to better ourselves in some way or improve and help our friends, families, colleagues, and the environments we work within?

This type of self-awareness drives an introspective approach to our lives that gives us a better chance to navigate and elevate ourselves. I know it has helped me tremendously in my own life. With just a few minutes each night, check in and ask if your actions aligned with your values for the day. Did you strengthen or weaken your moral fiber?

Perhaps you realize you faltered, and your moral fiber was weakened. That's OK. It happens. This process isn't about laying blame or feeling guilty. It's about always observing as well as arming ourselves with greater information and insight so we can make the right choices that align with our core values and the person we want to be.

For example, I have always had the desire to be physically healthy. But losing weight for me has always been a challenge as I constantly fluctuate. Granted, I may eat an extra serving of fries or chocolate that I know I should have passed, but I ate them. Rather than dwell on the decision, I've learned to forgive myself. At the same time, I take responsibility and accountability for this action, which empowers me to make a different choice the next day.

That's the power of engaging in this type of self-awareness; it helps us to catch ourselves prior to hitting that slippery slope. We must learn to question our every intent against our core values, which requires daily practice.

Below are just a few questions I use during my five-minute check-in:

- Did I act from my core values?
- What words did I use in my conversations?
- Did I sincerely listen to what people said to me?
- Does my self-interest align with my core values?
- Did I speak and act out from anger, greed, or ignorance?
- Did my actions have any impact on my environment and the people around me?
- Did I allow one of the four behavioral diseases (detraction, discrimination, deception, and doubt) to weave into my actions? Or did someone behave in one of those ways to me?

This is only a sample of the types of questions you can ask. All that matters is that your questions generate a deep introspection into your actions, so you gain critical insight into the type of moral footprint you're leaving in your business environment.

When you start practicing this type of reflection and awareness for five minutes a day, you'll find that you begin to train your mind to become accustomed to this heightened awareness. Those five minutes at the end of the day may turn into ten or fifteen minutes. And then those minutes at the end of the day may turn into minutes used during the course of your workday. Over time and with practice, you'll notice your awareness becomes heightened in a moment, for example, during a meeting. When this occurs, you're able to shift your actions and reactions in real time.

"To me, self-awareness is the ability to be in a moment and to recognize when you're doing something right, and also when you're doing something wrong, so you can correct the behavior if necessary," says Steven Guggenheimer, corporate vice-president and chief evangelist at Microsoft.[15]

In addition, practicing heightened awareness gives us

15   Guggenheimer, interview.

a greater opportunity to address what we may perceive to be as minor but others perceive to be as significant. It can be a great tool to better connect with ourselves and the people around us.

As Steven Guggenheimer continued to share with me, "I'm conscious of my body language, for example, like are my arms folded and crossed? Am I sitting in a way that might make people think I'm angry or mad versus relaxed? Or when I write e-mails, I put lots of happy faces in them, which may sound silly, but early in my career, I wrote short, terse e-mails that led people to think I was mad at them. I wasn't. To me, I was just being quick and direct, but it came across wrong, so I use happy faces to show people, 'Hey, I'm not mad, but here's my answer.'"[16]

## READING THE TEA LEAVES

We can also use our enhanced self-awareness skills to calm our minds, which allows us to observe our environments more closely. When we can calm our minds, it's like a camera on a grounded tripod. We are able to look at all vantage points in a balanced and equivocal way. We are better able to take in everything we see and feel around us. We absorb all the details of a room, the people in it including ourselves, how we're feeling, and what we're

16  Ibid.

thinking—all without judgment. It's like being an observer, attentive, watching, and living that moment. When we do this, we are practicing mindfulness, a state of active and open attention to the present.[17]

I practice this awareness before I go into a business meeting and the moment I enter any room. As a business leader, I'm used to high-level negotiations, so when I enter a room, the first thing I do is pause to get a feel and a sense for the energy in the room. *Ngön she'* in Tibetan means "heightened awareness," which is what I'm practicing. How many of us have walked into a meeting "feeling" the room, knowing what someone's thinking before shaking his or her hand? Some people call this intuition; others call it gut instinct. I call it being aware, and in business, it gives you a competitive advantage.

When I enter a room, I know most people have an agenda they want to push. And most people like to hear themselves talk, so I take a moment to listen to what they're saying and what they are not saying. Yes, it takes patience and discipline to not respond right away. However, you'll pinpoint the biggest influencers because your awareness will help you to identify the smallest nuances. For example, I was in a negotiation with two large companies in a

---

17  Psychology Today, "Mindfulness," accessed September 24, 2016 (https://www.psychologytoday.com/basics/mindfulness).

small conference room. By our design, the room had no windows and was sterile like a hospital room with the temperature set low. Our team was going to intentionally walk in late, as our goal was to make the others uncomfortable.

As we walked in, the leaders of the other company were waiting. Calm and patient, these Asian businessmen looked at us as they stood. We exchanged names, roles, and titles. After shaking hands, the youngest of the other Asian contingent politely said they would like to conduct the meeting in a more comfortable setting. His manager backed him. We, of course, pushed back, but the young man and his manager were adamant that if we didn't move the location of the meeting, the deal was off. They read the room and us. They knew this deal was a multi-million-dollar opportunity for our team, so we'd be forced to oblige their request.

When you harness this level of self-awareness and hypervigilance in your surroundings and the present moment, you'll maneuver through environments like these Asian businessmen.

## RAW AND REAL

Often, we shy away from a closer inspection of our motivations, intentions, actions, thoughts, and emotions because we're quick to judge ourselves and others. There was an interesting study done years ago that highlighted the tendency we have to place high standards for how others should act and behave, but when it comes to ourselves, we're apt to justify our own actions.

In a *U.S. News & World Report* survey, Americans were asked whether certain celebrities were likely to go to heaven when they passed away. Fifty-two percent of respondents said "yes" for former president Bill Clinton, while basketball legend Michael Jordan and Mother Teresa had 64 percent and 72 percent, respectively. But the individual who won the majority of respondents' yea votes was "yourself." A whopping 89 percent of survey respondents believed they were going to heaven.[18]

In my experience, this gap between our expectations of others and our assessments of ourselves prevents us from doing the deep introspection that I'm talking about. If we find that we've come up short in our behavior with other people, we'll harshly judge ourselves, perhaps believing we failed. "One barrier to true self-awareness and being honest with ourselves is the inability for many of us to forgive ourselves for our actions and motivations," explains Nien-hê Hsieh of Harvard Business School.[19]

18   "Oprah: A Heavenly Body," *U.S. News & World Report*, March 31, 1997, p. 18.

19   Hsieh, interview.

"At times, I'm afraid to really confront my motivations for why I acted or am acting a certain way," he says. "We need to look at what we did and why and acknowledge when it is wrong or when we wish we had acted differently. And then we need to forgive ourselves for those actions. However, true forgiveness is not a free pass. The point is if we can't forgive, we may be afraid to introspect. Forgiveness allows us to make real change."[20]

We also avoid the deep introspection because the victim mentality is deeply embedded in many of our mindsets. We may have been conditioned to deflect and blame the environments we're working in or the people we're working with for why we're compromising our values. It's easy to not take accountability. It's easy to tell ourselves that if the environment was better, if the people around us acted better and had better values, then we'd act differently, too. The truth is, the only element we can control is ourselves. And by looking closely at our own values and how we're acting, we can then make the necessary adjustments.

Self-awareness is about being constructive, not destructive by judging and blaming ourselves. We've all behaved in ways we wish we could have a do-over, or if faced with similar situations, we hope we'd handle them differently.

20   Ibid.

Ironically, our greatest strength is letting go and knowing that we all fail and make mistakes.

By practicing self-awareness, we begin to unveil our core values and what's important to us in our work life. It also helps us to begin the process of deep inquiry into our motivations, behaviors, thoughts, and emotions. Through this door, we also become more aware of our surroundings, and we begin to break free and elevate ourselves from the influence of the three poisons and toxic environments and people.

"Self-awareness is a precondition for moral development," Professor Sucher told me.[21] "It is a necessary (but not sufficient) condition to enable the noticing, discernment, and understanding of situations one is in, or the ability to notice, discern, and understand the behavior of other people and oneself. One can be morally judgmental without being self-aware, but the judgment will be flawed because the individual will not be able to reflect upon the thoughts, feelings, responses, and assumptions that she brings into a situation. I believe that moral development is a conscious act of self-cultivation, a striving to respond and behave in morally beneficial ways."[22]

---

21  Sucher, interview.

22  Ibid.

Lucy Hur, senior vice-president for partner resources at Starbucks uses awareness and self-awareness on a daily basis and credits those skills as part of the reason she has succeeded in her twenty-four years in the corporate world. "Being in the human resources space has taught me there are always different vantage points, and it is up to us to seek to understand and learn from every lens," she says.

"Understanding each person's intent, the various filters and interpretation that exist are critical when making a decision or recommendation. Awareness and self-awareness requires empathy and humility, which helps to rip our blindfolds off and to make us more approachable as we engage with each other. This results in more constructive and collaborative dialogues, which fosters better outcomes."[23]

The biggest difference between how I behave now compared to earlier in my career comes down to self-awareness. Before, I quickly reacted to situations, experiences, and my environments without any clear understanding of my motivations and thoughts. Like many business leaders, I let anger, greed, and ignorance take ahold of me, triggering a trade-off with my core values in certain situations.

In the past, I made some decisions I thought were right

23   Lucy Hur, interview by author, June 9, 2016.

even though my conscience pulled at me. At times, it was easier for me to wear a blindfold. So many of us in the corporate world have been, or are in, this position. Many of us have thought we were doing the right thing, only to learn that we have been mindlessly wandering.

After meeting the Dalai Lama, I learned we all have choices. As a result, we all must take accountability regardless of the influences in our lives. We can choose to slide that slippery slope of silencing our core values or we can act on them. We do have the choice to act from our inner voice.

Today, thankfully, I'm more in control of my thoughts and emotions because I've made building my moral fiber a priority. I'm more self-aware of my core values, what motivates me, the environment I work in, the people I work with, and my behaviors than ever before.

When I met the Dalai Lama for the first time, I knew it wasn't luck or by chance. It was a universal crossing, an opportunity for me to change the course of my life. It was an opportunity I seized, and I quickly gravitated to learn more about Buddhism and the Buddha. The Buddha is a being who attained complete purification of mind, speech, and body to reach a state of enlightenment. The Buddha reminds us that every one of us has the potential to reach enlightenment and become a Buddha, too. It's a given that everyone has a seed of Buddhahood (a subtle consciousness), and through the practice of deep meditation and virtuous actions, it can gradually be transformed to pure consciousness.

This opportunity to become a Buddha exists for us today, just as the opportunity to transform how we act in business exists for us today, too. It's not too late if we have acted unethically, compromised our values, or lost ourselves. The opportunity exists to be authentic, upfront, apologetic, forgiving, and to take accountability for our past actions and the actions of today.

As the Dalai Lama says, "I am not promoting Buddhism. I am promoting human values."[24]

When we take responsibility for our actions, it shows everybody in the company, from management to subordinates, that we are human, self-aware, and willing to work on ourselves and our performance. That simple act of humility and responsibility attracts others. They relate to you because everyone has been in the same spot at one time or another in their careers.

When we start taking responsibility for our actions

---
24  Craig, *The Pocket Dalai Lama*, 17.

(thoughts and emotions, too), the desire to be authentic and real in all our actions takes hold. Authenticity is the seed of our consciousness. This is what allows us to grow and strengthen our moral fiber—what returns us to the core of who we are.

By returning to our core, by rediscovering those inherent values within ourselves and acting in ways that temper the three poisons within us, we get a second chance—a second chance to succeed in business and in life by being true to ourselves. "Morality is not merely—or even principally—determining the right thing to do in specific instances," says Michael Wheeler, Harvard Business School. "Rather it entails who we want to be and what kind of life we want to lead."[25]

Once we know what our core values are, we can begin to put them into practice, which is what I'll show you in the next chapter.

---

25   Michael Wheeler and Julianna Pillemer, "Moral Decision-Making: Reason, Emotion & Luck," Harvard Business School, November 16, 2010, p. 16.

# THE LOCKER ROOM

Every morning after my one-hour cardio workout, I would walk into the muggy locker room, grab my towel, and then head to the shower. The smell of sweat from middle-aged, white-collar businessmen making well over six figures always dampened the room.

Most men would go in and out of the locker room, while some would constantly moan about their work, wives, bosses, the stock market, their golf games, and more. They all had great careers, drove fancy cars, traveled the world while their wives got manicures-pedicures, and sent their children to private schools.

Many of them were overweight, overpaid, and overworked.

No one appeared happy, but they found comfort and camaraderie in their shared suffering and the negativity that bounced off the walls. They all lived and worked in toxic environments, but none of them were aware of it.

Meanwhile, there was "old-school Oscar," all smiles with gray hair and wrinkles from the Arizona sun. Oscar was a retired maintenance engineer who worked at a large aircraft manufacturer for almost thirty years. Oscar worked part time as a janitor picking up towels and cleaning the toilets and sinks at the gym. He rarely said more than "Hello" or "Good day, sir," yet he knew everyone by name and was always respectful. I can't remember a time when I didn't see him smiling.

One morning, I stopped Oscar and asked why he worked at the gym. "Shawn, this place makes me happy."

That didn't make sense to me. How could a man in his seventies be happy listening and looking after arrogant self-serving jerks?

Oscar was a recovering alcoholic who had lost his wife to cancer. After enduring such heartache and suffering, wouldn't he rather be relaxing in the Bahamas? For reasons that baffled and confused me, Oscar said his job gave him meaning and purpose. For some time, Oscar had enjoyed retirement lounging on a sandy beach, but it got old and he needed to have a purpose.

Even more astonishing to me, Oscar said in this job, he was the happiest he'd ever been. "Happiness came from my own suffering, Shawn," Oscar told me. "Feeling sorry for my losses was easy, but it only led to my emptiness. After so many years, my pain became my window, and I began to practice concentration for long periods of time."

This intense concentration led Oscar to clarity of himself and his life, and it altered his perspective of other people. I latched on to the word *perspective*, wondering if it takes a lifetime, or to be a recovering addict who lost everything, to gain the right perspective. After losing his wife, Oscar shared with me that he had to train his mind to be compassionate because his anger would take over his mind. He was angry at God and everyone around him. He blamed himself and everything for the loss of his wife. He learned to embrace the anger but was wise not to fuel himself with it as hate would have led to destructive behaviors.

Every time he would get angry, Oscar would practice what he called "outside living," similar to an out-of-body experience. He would imagine that he was watching himself in the room from high above. Doing this regularly helped him detach and elevate him from these angry situations. More importantly, it gave him focus, a calmness of mind, and allowed for clarity to seep in so he could better concentrate and take a more mindful approach versus overreacting.

I listened to Oscar and watched the men rush around us. I wondered, *Were these white-collared businessmen ever going to see the world through eyes like Oscar's? Were their perspectives ever going to evolve beyond their greed and negativity?*

One morning, Oscar lifted my towel and handed it to me. As I reached for it, he yanked it back, teasing and laughing loudly like a child, drowning out the morning background griping. He was happy, content, and at peace with where he was in life.

We can all learn something from Oscar.

CHAPTER 5

# BALANCING SELF IN ETHICAL DISCIPLINE

---

SILA *DEF.* ETHICAL CONDUCT

After a twelve-hour flight and three espressos, my colleagues and I walked through the glass doors of our Paris office ready to make a presentation on field resourcing to the vice-president (VP) of the company and his leadership team. Eight months into my new role, I was eager to impress.

We nervously rode the elevator, knowing this presentation would take us to the next level in our careers; however, the question looming over us was whether that move would be up or down. I waited in the hallway with a glass of water in one hand and a pen and laptop clutched in the other. The wide doors opened, and we were directed to stand before a U-shaped conference table littered with paper, computers, and half-empty cups of coffee.

People were laughing as we walked in. Were they laughing loudly from the previous presentation? Slowly, silence overtook the crowd, as the VP turned and signaled for me to begin. I moved to prepare our slide presentation. "No slides," the VP hollered. "Walk me through your presentation without them."

I turned and stared, instantly flustered and caught off-guard. I did as the VP instructed, but no more than five minutes into what was to be a one-hour presentation, the VP interrupted me. "Your proposal lacks substance, and I don't want to waste anyone's time listening to this," he said. "Thank you. Now please leave."

We were dismissed and cast aside in the VP's rush to judgment. Shocked, I was unable to respond and unsure of how to react to him.

My eyes darted around the table as I caught the leadership team laughing. Only two women looked at me with a hint of compassion, but they remained silent. I felt disgusted and judged without merit. Did I make a wrong decision taking this new role? I felt my career spiraling down in this one moment, and I was helpless toward my teammates.

With nothing left to say, my team and I turned to walk out, when suddenly Chris, part of the leadership team, spoke. "Why are you making a decision without listening to what Shawn has to say after you invited him here?" he asked the VP in a moderate tone. The room grew quiet as the laughter ceased. Chris smiled and said, "I understand Shawn is new to this role and that his management team is seeking our feedback on this proposal."

The VP's face flashed red with fury. You could see his internal dialogue spin "Who was this Chris, this young child questioning me, a twenty-year veteran?" But Chris's act and his willingness to speak out on a situation he believed was unfair called attention to the VP's shameful and ignorant approach. The *approach* Chris used jarred the VP out of his anger and ignorance because he turned to me and asked that I continue the presentation.

I believe it was *how* Chris engaged the VP that made all the difference. Chris reminded the team of the company's core value of respect, showcasing the VP's deplorable actions. More importantly, Chris fueled a spirit of collaboration in a calm and collective way between two management teams across the globe by stating my management team was looking for the VP's feedback.

As a result, our recommendation was accepted, and the VP apologized, saying he should have let me speak. After the meeting, we successfully rolled out our plan, and I received an outstanding annual review.

But none of this would have been possible without Chris's powerful act of compassion and wisdom that influenced everyone, most importantly, the VP. Chris could have remained silent, but he saw something he believed was wrong and unfair. He stood up and acted on what he believed was right, despite the threat to his position; many people won't speak out in a public setting like that against their leader for fear of retaliation. But Chris willingly placed his career on the line to push against the herd mentality.

I've known Chris for a long time and he's compassionate by nature. He values respect and fairness. That day, his actions aligned with his values. He acted with courage, being true to his character. He could have responded with anger to the VP—I know I wanted to. But instead, he chose a different path, a path paved with compassion and wisdom instead of anger and ignorance.

And we were all the better for it.

Chris's story is important because within it lies the secret to overcoming the three poisons of anger, greed, and ignorance. That secret is to balance the three poisons by counteracting them with compassion, gratitude, and wisdom.

Using compassion, gratitude, and wisdom to manage the three poisons is a similar approach to what Buddhists call the Middle Way. The first, and one of the most important teachings the Buddha gave after he reached enlightenment, was about the Middle Way.[1] The Middle Way is a path of moderation between the extremes of our world, the sensual indulgences of pleasure and the deprivation and self-mortification of pain. The Buddha taught that if you avoided the extremes in life and tamed your emotions and thoughts, you could walk the Middle Way and end your suffering.

Much of our suffering in business stems from compromising our values as we give in, at times, to the emotions of anger, greed, and ignorance. However, when we choose to move away from those emotions and move toward compassion, gratitude, and wisdom, we create balance and begin to walk our own Middle Way.

---

1   "Setting in Motion the Wheel of Truth," Buddha Net, accessed February
    28, 2016 (http://www.buddhanet.net/bp_sut17.htm).

When we do this, we find that the toxic environments that influenced us begin to crumble. We navigate complex and challenging situations easier and more authentically, and over time, we begin to elevate.

## MANAGING THE POISONS

In the following three stories, I share how I learned to counteract the three poisons by using the antidotes of compassion, gratitude, and wisdom. The key to each of these stories was that I was using my self-awareness to recognize what was happening in the moment, or shortly after, which unlocked the power to change my behavior.

### TURNING ANGER INTO COMPASSION

*8:00 a.m.*

My day started on a team conference call. Sipping coffee, I listened as my colleague informed me he hadn't finished his deliverable. His delay meant that my portion of the project was delayed, my time line screwed up, and my commitment to management thrown off from our original plan. My anger flared at this news, and I let it roar, belittling my colleague in front of our team.

When the call ended, I paused to reflect on the meeting

# CRAVING COFFEE CALMLY

I'm a coffee addict, so every morning around 7:30 a.m. I go to my favorite place, Peet's Coffee & Tea. Usually the line is short, a couple of people at the most, so I'm quickly in and out. But one morning, I found a long line out the door. With an early meeting, I was less than thrilled to wait in line for my regular cup of coffee.

But I craved that coffee badly. I *needed* to have it, and I needed to have it from *that* coffee shop.

As I stood in line, behind what had to be twenty new faces, frustration blanketed me. I looked at the folks in front of me, at the barista, at everyone in line and I thought, *What is taking so long?* Like a child, my frustration turned to anger over having to wait. Then I noticed other thoughts that drifted across my mind as I gazed at the new people standing between me and my coffee. *What is* he *wearing? What are* they *talking about? Who are* these *new people and what are* they *doing here?*

I was lost to my anger, which had turned to ignorance as I stood making ludicrous judgments and comments about human beings whom I knew nothing about. The three poisons raged within me.

Years ago, I would have continued to stand there in my anger and ignorance, and then more than likely, I would have brought it to the office. I would have easily acted or made decisions from the poisons. But this time, I broke the pattern. I took a deep breath and became more self-aware of my emotions and thoughts. I checked in and noticed I was angry and was making ignorant judgments. Once I noticed all of this, then I had a choice. I could hold on to the anger and ignorance, or I could choose to let it go and instead try to embrace compassion and wisdom.

I chose to let the running dialogue in my head stop, to shut myself up, and to trade my anger and ignorance for a heightened awareness of my surroundings. I chose to stop my mind from wandering and to stop the harsh judgments. I even chose to stop thinking about how much I wanted my coffee—and I *really* wanted that coffee—and to make it to my upcoming meeting on time. In fact, I stopped myself from thinking all together and focused on listening and noticing my surroundings.

The two people in front of me were of French descent. I never would have noticed or associated myself with them before. But I overheard them discussing French cuisine. It was actually an interesting conversation because they were talking about opening a French bakery nearby.

Then I did something that my younger self, before I had awakened my core values, wouldn't have done: I reached out to them. I said I couldn't help but overhear their conversation and wanted to know more about their business idea. We ended up conversing in line together, and I learned more about them, their idea, and even mutual acquaintances.

By becoming aware of myself and the environment, I transformed my ill emotion into compassion and wisdom. This led to a wonderful, thought-provoking conversation with two strangers. None of this would have been possible had I remained gripped by the three poisons.

With my thoughts, I could have created a toxic environment at the coffee shop. In fact, I was already creating one until I flipped it around. Today, I have a new French bakery where I go to enjoy my morning coffee.

and my behavior. That's when it hit me: I fed into the anger. I dug deeper, asking why I got so angry. Why did I race to yell and belittle my colleague? I honestly answered the questions. First, I was attached to meeting my time line for delivering my piece of the project. However, the time line was adjustable, and that reason didn't justify my actions.

Second, and the more relevant answer, was that I was angry at myself, not my colleague who bore the brunt of my tirade. The night before, I spent caring for my sick daughter, and I hadn't slept much. When I started the meeting, I was tired, unhappy, and angry from the night's events. But that was on me, not my colleague. During the call, I wasn't in control of my emotions and I allowed my anger to fester and scale rapidly. I behaved inappropriately and simply overreacted to the situation.

As I went through this exercise of introspection, I began to feel more compassion for my colleague. I realized that next time, when I feel the emotion of anger rise, instead of lashing out, I need to recognize it and take a breath. I need to gather more information and deal with unexpected news with greater maturity. Next time, I would try to better understand the root cause of his delay. Was there something going on in his life that prevented him from getting his part done? Was there something the team could have helped him with so we meet our deadlines together?

Buddhism teaches that we often become angry because we use only one lens to view our experiences, when in reality, multiple perspectives exist. Everything is fluid and impermanent. Everything and everyone is interdependent. There is a cause and effect to everything, and understanding the cause of your anger can help you to calm it or at least control it. Often, we're not angry out of malicious intent. I certainly wasn't. It was because of misconceptions, distorted views, attachment, and deflection from what was really troubling me.

In my youth and in my early career, I often used anger to fight anger, which eliminated any chance for learning or growing. As Buddhists would say, slaying a corpse is all I accomplished.

Today, when I'm faced with similar situations that invoke the emotion of anger, instead of immediately reacting and then regretting how I behaved, I better anticipate when the anger is about to rise. As I talked about in chapter 4, when we can identify what we're feeling and thinking in the moment through self-awareness, introspection, and mindfulness, we have the power to adjust our behaviors accordingly. This is how we can manage the emotion of anger.

## FROM GREED TO GRATITUDE

I was in a major West Coast city having just closed one of the biggest deals for our company. We had formed a new partnership with one of the local area vendors that had the technological capability of working with us at the price point we wanted. This was a multimillion-dollar deal for both my company and the vendor.

With the deal secured, I turned my attention to courting and making sure Jerry, the CEO of the vendor, and his VPs were happy. Like most sales executives, I had an expense account to take our partners and clients out for meals and drinks. Jerry chose an expensive steakhouse for our celebration.

I've had hundreds of dinners like these over my career, but few have pushed the limits of my expense account like Jerry. His first order consisted of three ounces of expensive caviar and drinks. Clearly, he wanted to have a good time and was accustomed to having fun. We left with close to a $4,000 dinner tab. I was astounded at the excess and wanton disregard for price. I figured we'd call it a night, but Jerry had other ideas. He called his driver to take us to a "cigars and brandy" private club, except the private club had more than brandy and cigar smoke. I watched in stunned silence as one of the VPs pulled white powder out of his suit pocket.

"Do you want a hit?" the VP asked me.

"No. I absolutely *don't* want a hit," I replied, annoyed.

As the night progressed, my team and I grew more uncomfortable with the use of drugs, the never-ending fountain of liquor, and the haze of cigar smoke that wafted over us. I sipped my drink and watched feeling more conflicted as the minutes ticked past. We weren't in a business environment per se, and these guys weren't thinking about business, only about having a great time and partying. However, I couldn't separate the business side of these men from their partying ways. Questions sped across my mind. Should I make a judgment about their characters based on what I was witnessing from this night out? Do I judge their ability to get the job done or whether these were the types of people we needed and wanted to work with based on this situation? Do I voice my concerns right now about our partnership? Do I voice my concerns about their behaviors?

After watching the blatant disregard for dinner expenses, the drug use, and the over-the-top partying, I was worried about this partnership with Jerry's company. But I also knew we needed them to successfully execute on our new project with the customer. We had very few options for vendors that possessed the technological capability to interface with ours at our preferred price point in the area. If we didn't work with Jerry's company, we'd jeopardize our ability to successfully execute on the project.

I was mindful of the situation and the possible results from any action I took in that moment. Turning inward to my values, I decided the best decision was to walk away for the night without saying anything to Jerry. I couldn't say anything without compromising our project, but I was also reluctant to compromise my values, or those of my team, to remain in an unhealthy environment. Excusing myself from the table, I called a cab and asked the others on my team if they wanted to join me. Not surprisingly, they all did.

After reflecting more on the situation, I decided to reopen the bidding process for the vendor who could deploy our services. What I saw that night with Jerry's team were red flags. I was worried their high-flying ways would bleed into the work environment, impact our team, and risk our contract and relationship with the customer. These were risks I couldn't take. In the end, we chose another vendor and were extremely successful.

Instead of acting immediately on my emotional state or thoughts that evening, I waited until I could act from a position that was true to my values. I removed myself from the environment to gain greater perspective on what I witnessed and to reflect and evaluate whether this was the right partner for us. I grabbed the emotion of greed and turned it on its back. I focused on factors such as whether this partner was right for my team and the potential impact on other key stakeholders including the customer.

We all want to have a good time and indulge in some of the finer things in life, but what Jerry and his team displayed was taken to an extreme. Their appetite wasn't satiated and their excessive behavior ultimately led to their losing a lucrative contract.

"The thing with greed is, it is never enough," says Joanne Harrell, Board of Regents, University of Washington and former board director of REI. "I've seen greed manifest itself multiple times, with people who have long corporate work histories and have amassed considerable wealth after decades spent climbing up the corporate ladder. Despite their success, some of these people remain unsatisfied and unfulfilled due to always wanting *more*. The key is to reach the point of having *enough*, which entails recognizing our blessings and reaching a point of satiation or fullness. Otherwise, we'll always be unhappy and unfulfilled despite having abundance"[2]

I balance my own greed with gratitude by looking at my life through a different lens. I see everything that I have and what others don't have. I look at the people and the companies I work with, and I feel grateful I get to work with talented and wise people. I look at the relationships in my life and my precious daughter. I still want to drive strong business results, and I do, and I still want to attain greater wealth and enjoy the pleasures of the world, but I'm more aware, balanced, and grateful for everything and everyone in my life. More importantly, my drive to

2   Harrell, interview.

attain greater opportunity and well-being is not at the cost of another. Instead, I now make an effort to ensure the same opportunity exists for all.

We can still want things in life, good salaries, nice homes, and great vacations, but we must balance those things with gratitude and a mindset that our actions should focus on improving the greater good.

## IGNORANCE GIVES WAY TO WISDOM

Partnerships make or break a business, especially in the technology world where no company can succeed alone. In this example, we had three major components of an ecosystem delivering goods to a customer: (1) a technology company, (2) the vendor that deploys the technology company's services, and (3) the suppliers. To succeed, all three parties had to work collaboratively, but that doesn't always happen.

This was the case on an account I managed. Each party played a vital role and was necessary to produce the product and the solution for our customers. This wasn't a small project; we're talking millions of dollars. But no one acted like a team, and collaboration was nonexistent. Most of the teams' interactions with one another consisted of judging the other companies. It felt like I was on a hamster wheel. Every day, someone pointed a finger and blamed someone else for mistakes and missed deadlines. People were stuck and acted from ignorance and preconceived notions.

It wasn't long before I realized we were on the cusp of failing to deliver the product and solution. So my first act was to acutely listen to everyone and take detailed notes on who spoke and what was said. Once I assessed everyone, next I asked simple questions when I heard an ignorant comment. On the spot, I'd call the person out, but I was careful to avoid being or sounding angry or upset. This was out of a genuine desire to gather more information. If David blamed or judged another team or team member, I'd ask him directly why he made the comment.

I wanted to understand everyone's intentions and motivations behind their commentary. As I've said, most people aren't coming from a malicious place; they're misguided. Most of the team members shared the same motivation: fear. Everyone was fearful of what the other person was going to do. They didn't trust the other team would get their portion of the job done correctly, which in turn made people fearful about their ability to complete their leg of the project. It was fear and insecurity that drove the finger-pointing and blaming, and that was inhibiting any productivity and efficiency from happening.

I could have easily joined the ignorance wagon, jumping to conclusions and false pretenses. Instead, I chose to gather more information and facts (what I now consider vantage points) to achieve greater awareness of the situation. Once I had greater clarity, I brought all the stakeholders together in one room. I noticed that most of the companies spoke negatively about one another when they were alone. It was like having someone gossip about you, but when you see them, they smile and clap you on the shoulder as if nothing's wrong. Instead of playing that game, I called everyone from the three companies into one room to bring attention to the grievances and fears.

I looked at company A and told them they're making claims because they're afraid company C would screw up. Then I'd turn to company C and tell them that they're fearful that company B was going to miss a deadline.

I replayed all the fears and insecurities back to each stakeholder because we needed to bring truth and transparency to the situation. By getting everyone in the room and becoming raw and real about our thoughts, feelings, and concerns, we overcame the ignorant assumptions and misconceptions.

This approach took significant time, but it brought trust into a deceitful environment. Trust is a critical element in business. You need to be able to trust your team, your partners, your clients, and yourself. Having awareness and wisdom helps to forge that trust. By counteracting ignorance with greater awareness and wisdom, we built a transparent and trusted environment for our teams to work in. The result is that we flourished. We enjoyed real collaboration, hit deadlines, and knocked objectives off the list. This is one way we can manage the poison of ignorance.

## ACT: BALANCING THE POISONS DAILY

*Change only takes place through action, not through meditation and prayer alone.*

— DALAI LAMA[3]


Each of these stories highlight awareness as the lens I needed to detect the right emotion to seek balance and positive outcomes. Every day, a myriad of emotions live inside of us. The question is whether we'll act from the poisons or if we'll counter them with their antidotes leveraging our values.

Remember in chapter 3 when I shared what former Enron

---

3    Dean E. Murphy, "Do More Than Pray," *Los Angeles Times*, December 9, 1999 (http://articles.latimes.com/1999/dec/09/news/mn-42064).

VP (and internal whistle-blower) Sherron Watkins discussed about the frog sitting in the cold water getting ready to be boiled? Awareness becomes your foresight in detecting when the water becomes lukewarm. It allows you to gauge the temperature and act with mindfulness *before* emotions begin to boil and to cause destructive behaviors in and around you.

In business, all emotions, including anger, greed, and ignorance, are always present, and they need to be dialed appropriately given the situation. For example, catching your employee stealing from you would make you angry— so angry that you may overreact at that moment in time without all the information. Detecting the emotion before it flares and you act on it is critical because you want to understand all the vantage points before acting. Getting all the facts before reacting requires greater patience, strength, and tolerance than just simply lashing out.

What if you learn that your employee was just borrowing something or was asked by one of your managers to move its location? If you had immediately reacted and lashed out in anger, now you'd feel foolish and appear ignorant. However, if you take a mindful approach, check the anger first, and then seek out more information, you can respond appropriately based on your values. If it turns out the employee was stealing, then you can hold him or her accountable with strict consequences that reinforces your values and sets a fair tone in the organization.

Yes, these emotions can cause immense harm. However, it's the actions we take without awareness, the uncontrolled emotions, and responses that lead to a far worse outcome that causes us to compromise our values. "Psychologists view anger as a natural emotion that can act as an indicator or a warning that a moral breach occurred," explains Lisa Felice, PhD, organizational psychologist and consultant. "Anger can be your friend, but it's important to get to the root of what's causing that feeling and then address that."[4]

Dialing our emotions back takes practice and that comes through self-awareness and mindfulness. This balanced state allows us to calibrate our emotions against our moral compass before acting on them. In short, we need to understand the source of these emotions so we can channel them more constructively.

This happened to business leader Joanne Harrell who turned her experiences with a toxic boss into something positive. An executive VP tapped Joanne to give a presentation to the senior management team on a topic her manager, Bob, was leading. Her involvement and

4    Felice, interview.

presentation angered Bob. So shortly after the meeting, he called Joanne into his office saying he wanted to give her feedback. He told her there was a perception in the office among the upper management team that Joanne wasn't assertive enough in meetings. He went on to explain that if she wanted to move up in the company, she'd have to change the way she was perceived.

"I was surprised, hurt, and upset by what he said," remembers Joanne. "I went back to my desk puzzled and thought into the evening about each of the scenarios where I had presented to upper management. I knew I had done a good job because the feedback I received at those times was positive. My instincts told me to find out more about Bob's comments, so that's what I did."

Joanne went to Bob's boss, Chuck, the division manager, and asked him about the feedback Bob had shared, gently probing to understand the statements she'd heard about how she was perceived. Chuck was uncomfortable and adamant that he didn't say anything close to the feedback Joanne had heard and that that his perception of her was quite positive. Next, Joanne went a level higher than Chuck, to the department head. He said that what she'd heard had been twisted and didn't reflect his confidence in her abilities and appreciation of her thoughtful and considerate engagement style.

In a few conversations, Joanne was able to clarify what was said about her and to understand the motives driving her manager's remarks. Instead of allowing anger or hurt to drive her actions, Joanne detached and instead, sought the truth. "My boss had several personal issues, and I happened to be in front of him as a manifestation of his insecurities. I seemed to be the perfect target for his anger, but what he didn't realize was that I was motivated by a strong desire to understand the feedback and seek full insight (truth) into what I had been told."[5]

Joanne's story is a perfect example of how to turn your disappointment, anger, and pain into something positive. The next time you find yourself on the receiving end of someone's tirade, remember Joanne's story. You don't have to fight anger with anger. Getting to the truth really will set you free.

Many leaders will tell you that sometimes showing anger can help to motivate their teams. Or sometimes our greed pushes us to achieve greater innovation, more productivity, and better outcomes. Even ignorance can benefit you if you're willing to admit what you don't know. For this to work, however, you need a keen awareness of yourself to help you to identify what emotion has arisen immediately. You'll also need strong introspection to help you

5    Harrell, interview.

to understand the origin of the emotion and an ability to evaluate the situation before determining whether to act from that emotion or to temper it with compassion, gratitude, or wisdom.

"Always be compassionate. Being angry or hard on people doesn't really help them grow. Being firm, clear, and direct is fair. But anger rarely is a good approach," says Steven Guggenheimer, corporate VP and chief evangelist at Microsoft. "The trick is to find the balance for where you should sit on each of those spectrums—anger or compassion—in every moment and determine whether that emotion, and your action connected to it, will add value to your organization and the people around you."[6]

Whenever I found myself in challenging situations, I used to react quickly, then spend half my time defending my decision and/or position. Today, I take a more mindful approach leveraging a three-step process I call ACT: accept, cloister, and temper.

ACT helps me to recognize, evaluate, and gain control over my emotions, especially the three poisons as well as other toxic emotions such as fear, pride, conceit, arrogance, jealousy, desire, lust, closed-mindedness, and

6   Guggenheimer, interview.

others. This ensures that whatever action I take is true to my values and who I am.

1.  **Accept the emotion that arises.** This isn't about judging or beating yourself up for what you feel, nor is it blaming a person or a situation for your feelings. This is simply an acknowledgment of what you feel and identifying that emotion, whether it's anger, envy, ignorance, hate, sadness, or something else. The more you practice embracing the emotions, the greater your awareness of them becomes.

2.  **Cloister and isolate the emotion.** Understand the cause and origin of each emotion. Isolate the poisons of anger, greed, and ignorance and dissect why they've arisen. When I became angry on the conference call, my colleague wasn't the root of that emotion. The real issue was personal. It was my lack of sleep having cared for my sick child that caused my irritation. I had deflected my emotion and behavior onto my colleague.

3.  **Temper the emotion with concentration and mindfulness.** In this step, you'd act on the emotion you've isolated. If you're feeling anger, then you'd temper it using compassion. If it's greed, then you'd use gratitude. If it's ignorance, then you'd turn toward wisdom.

Concentration and mindfulness is about consciously knowing what you're experiencing and then reinforcing your actions to align with your values and the way you want to be in the world. This is about ensuring the actions you take are intended, rather than abrupt and merely reactionary.

Of course, mastering ACT requires patience, tolerance, and resolve, and it will take time through daily practice before this process happens naturally.

Our actions, which stem from our emotions and behaviors, contribute to our environments either positively or negatively. "If one reacts to a situation in a negative way instead of in a tolerant way, not only is there no immediate benefit, but also a negative attitude and feeling is created which is the seed of one's future downfall," says the Dalai Lama.[7]

Robin O'Connell, executive VP at Uphold Incorporated, told me that we should try to determine how a decision will impact things in the next five minutes, the next five days, and the next five years.[8] It seems like a long time, but O'Connell's point is that our actions ripple in ways we cannot always see or expect, which should make us

7   The Dalai Lama, *Healing Anger*, 10.

8   Robin O'Connell, interview by author, September 29, 2015.

## MILITARY MINDFULNESS THROUGH ACT

Colonel Karl Walli (ret.), PhD, served more than twenty-five years in the United States Air Force. He can attest to the many times he had to lean on his compassion and core values while leveraging self-awareness to overcome tactical and strategic adversity in the military.

In one difficult situation, Col. Walli became very resentful of a superior officer who seemed more driven by a desire for promotion than by doing the "right things" for the mission and the unit's personnel. The military remains a very stratified environment where a disagreement with a superior has to be handled behind "closed doors," so that insubordination does not erode unit cohesion and command authority. Unfortunately, the adverse effect of not being able to openly state your opinion is that resentment often has no outlet, and it soon becomes psychologically toxic. Col. Walli's situation grew so bad that it almost ended in his separation from the military at an early age (unfortunately, this is a common outcome for many servicemen and servicewomen).

Although Col. Walli believes that the large majority of the military personnel who serve our country are intensely patriotic, a small minority are "careerists"—people who care more for promotion and professional advancement than for successfully accomplishing the mission for the common good. He refers to these individuals as "Paper Tigers," as they appear from their records and résumés to "walk on water" even though these individuals can seldom be counted on to perform the hard, often-menial tasks required to get the job done. As I have discussed earlier in the book, this type of deceptive behavior is a key indicator of a toxic environment.

What caused Col. Walli's early resentment was his quick attachment to people, mission goals, and strategic outcomes and his belief that others should share those same objectives and values. For Col. Walli, his core values centered on selflessness, patriotism, deep faith, and close interpersonal relationships with family, friends, and coworkers.

He always believed he had to be in control of the situation, whatever that situation, and to drive a successful outcome; his fear of failure was a never-ending cause of intense personal stress.

Over the years, he learned that the only control he had was within himself and that he could not control the Paper Tigers of the military world. In this self-realization, he began to look inward and focused on his thoughts, his actions, and his work-family life balance. He effectively leveraged an approach similar to ACT that used his core values as an "anchor" to make critical decisions and navigate through toxic environments and people.

Col. Walli believes giving oneself for his fellow man is the greatest and most noble purpose one can fulfill in life. "As an airman, I tried to use compassion to influence my decisions, and as an officer, I strived for balanced leadership that was anchored on my core values to execute decisions wisely," he says.

Col. Walli says that his values were profoundly influenced and forged growing up as a Catholic farm boy from a large family that embraced midwestern values such as selflessness, patriotism, deep faith, and close interpersonal relationships with your community. Like many, Col. Walli had his cultural hinges and societal strings, but the military allowed him to practice his core values daily. One of his greatest values that he strove to display and that he cherished in others was selflessness. He saw this in his faith as well as the air force and his military way of life.

"It is in the balance of our emotions, tempered by our core values where our individual path must lead," explains Col. Walli. "Too often, we get swayed in the extremes, moving from one emotion to the next. The goal is to cloister and seclude the emotion and balance it. Having this balance detaches us just enough to provide objectivity in our decision making to enable us to make rationale choices."[1]

---

1    Karl Walli, interview by author, December 3, 2016.

all more careful in the actions we take and the words we speak.

When you're used to reacting to situations without any awareness for your emotions, it's tough to suddenly identify them. For many of us, it's often an easier path to mimic the behaviors, especially those caused by the poisons, exuded by the environment. Like locusts, the poisons quickly replicate inside of us, caging our minds and making it harder to identify new, more positive approaches to resolving a situation. In the past, I would never have thought compassion—the polar opposite of anger—would be the countermeasure to anger. Acting on compassion while angry is not a natural and intuitive emotion for most of us, especially when we're gripped in a heightened state of hate and/or fear.

Hence, we must recondition our minds, but this takes knowing and acting on our values. It takes our willingness to engage in ethical discipline. As His Holiness the Dalai Lama states, "Ethical discipline is the indispensable means for mediating between the competing claims of my right to happiness and others' equal right."[9]

This requires knowing and *acting* on our values; it's using our moral fiber. It is this continuous practice that we bring

9   The Dalai Lama, Twitter Post, September 2, 2010, 1:34 a.m.

into everyday experiences that help mediate these competing claims with our fellow human beings.

Personally, I've used meditation to help me mediate the different emotions that arise and find balance leveraging ACT. For so long, I was reactive. Someone would say something to me, an e-mail would come through, or an event happened, and I just responded. I overreacted without any keen awareness of my feelings and thoughts and whether those actions opposed or supported my values. I needed a tool to help me recognize and balance all of this, and meditation worked for me.

Although in the beginning, it was difficult for me to practice, the more I did it, the easier it became. And the more I practiced, the more I recognized my emotions in real time such as during a conversation, when my inbox pinged with new e-mail, or while attending a meeting. Having this real-time perspective ensures that I'm acting on my core values, rather than being influenced by the poisons of anger, greed, and ignorance. This means that I no longer have a standoff between my core values and a potentially compromising situation.

Now, I meditate first thing in the morning every day to clear my mind.

Mary Gentile, director of Giving Voice to Values and professor of practice at the University of Virginia Darden School of Business, explained to me the power and benefits of clearing our minds:

> It's very stressful when people encounter value conflicts in their work. It raises emotions, and people will feel like it's an interruption in their lives. They're doing their work, they're pursuing their goals, and something happens that they wish didn't. They wish they never saw or experienced this situation, so they close their eyes tightly to get through it. They want to return to their job, but this leads people to deny the situation or to do what they believe is the wrong thing very quickly, hoping they won't have to think about the situation again.
>
> I've found, though, if you can recognize that these unavoidable situations will arise, that they are as much a part of business as they are of life, and if you can lower your emotion to remain centered and calm, then you can maintain a state of being, a state of mind, that allows you to tap into more options and your strengths.[10]

---

10  Gentile, interview.

I'm not saying you have to meditate or that it's the only way to help you to connect and identify your emotions. Only you know if meditation is effective for you. But if you're looking for tools to help, then I encourage you to give it a try. The key is to find a way to master and control your emotions and thoughts so that you aren't reacting to toxic situations unintentionally or unconsciously.

In the next chapter, I'm going to show you how knowing and acting on your values is possible in any situation.

## COURAGE COMES FROM LIVING A VALUE-BASED LIFE

Lucy Hur, senior VP for partner resources for Starbucks, has lived in the eye of the hurricane witnessing compromising situations throughout her twenty-four years in the human resource field. She credits her values of integrity, respect, kindness, learning, and hard work for giving her the strength and courage to survive the daily challenges.[1]

Her values have guided her and acted as a sounding board to help her navigate through tough situations. Her values have given her purpose, and by practicing her values daily, she's been able to walk through fearful or ambiguous situations at any given moment. She credits her strong values with giving her the confidence that the right outcome will always ensue, no matter how challenging the situation.

"I've always acted on my values, no matter the seniority of the person or situation," says Lucy.[2]

As a Korean immigrating to the United States when she was five years old, Lucy watched her parents work diligently to rebuild their lives (twice) with integrity. When her family was going through tough times, kindness and compassion knocked on their front door from friends, neighbors, and colleagues. Her Asian heritage and culture instilled in her to respect others and to value education and learning as a lifelong journey. Lucy embodies her parents' values, and she is not afraid of ever "rebuilding" or slaying fear with confidence to overcome any challenge.

Lucy is the real deal. I've seen her act on her values. She has no fear telling senior leaders if they have acted wrongly, but she always does this in a respectful and balanced way. Her approach is simple: be direct and real time in giving feedback, and always stay calm. Her fearlessness does not come from her values preaching to her but rather, from strengthening her moral fiber by knowing and acting on her values. Taking this approach has worked for Lucy as she has been extremely successful in her career all while being true to herself and her way of being and living her life.

"What is the worst thing that could happen to me by acting on my values?" she asks. "Sure, I could lose my job because I stood up for what is right, but then I can always get another job. Acting on my values allows me to be true to myself, and by doing so, I have more courage. It's liberating."

---

1   Hur, interview.

2   Ibid.

# CHAPTER 6

# SEEDING CORPORATE CONSCIOUSNESS

———

KARUNA *DEF.* COMPASSIONATE ACTION

In the end, our actions define us—individually, organizationally, culturally, and societally. And when we act, do we become more or less the person we desire to be? When we act, do we strengthen our moral fiber and drive positive energy and change into our organizations? When we act, is it done from our core values?

"I try and take the high road when faced with compromising situations," says Joe Gullo, business leader at Rambus.

"If and when I have stooped to questionable behavior in retaliation for how I was treated, it didn't work for me. It's not who I am. I wasn't being true to myself, my beliefs, and how I think. If you know who you are, then be who you are. You can't control how the people around you act, their thoughts, emotions, or values. But you can control yours."[1]

Joe makes it sound easy, doesn't he? I do know that when you strengthen your moral fiber by acting on your values, toxic environments won't trouble you. But how do you *really* act on your values? What does that look like? And what can you do, starting today, to identify and then act on your values, thus strengthening your moral fiber?

In this chapter, I share with you a methodology that I've used to help me align my values with my actions to strengthen my moral fiber. I've taken the liberty to leverage part of the book title, FIBER, as an acronym to better categorize and frame this five-step approach. Hopefully, this will also make it easier for you to remember the process.

This method helped me to not only be true to myself in business but to also drive greater outcomes for my company. It's something I regularly return to when faced with toxic environments, behaviors, situations, and people.

1   Gullo, interview.

In a way, I'm advocating that you make a lifestyle change. Or think of building your moral fiber like strength training. When you first start lifting weights, maybe you can bench press only sixty pounds, but as you make lifting a priority in your life and commit to training, your strength increases. Soon, you're bench pressing 90, then 120, then 150 pounds.

It's the same concept with building our moral fiber. Little by little, day by day, the more we train ourselves to identify and then act on our values, the stronger our moral fiber becomes. The stronger our moral fiber, the easier it is for us to navigate, change, and rise above the toxic environments, situations, and people that/who surround us.

At first, identifying and acting on our values may be uncomfortable, but if we don't consciously choose to strengthen our moral fiber, we risk compromising our values and ourselves. When this happens, our values become like trophies collecting dust on a mantel. We sit and stare at them, remembering the person we could have been and what we could have done in our life.

Even worse, by not acting on our values, we potentially contribute to self-deception, leading to greater toxicity and moral fading. As philosopher Edmund Burke said, "the only thing necessary for the triumph of evil is for good men to do nothing."[2]

FIBER is meant to help make acting on our core values more feasible and to ensure we don't leave them sitting on a mantel. This tool combines many of the elements that I wrote about in the previous chapters.

## FIBER: A SIMPLE FIVE-STEP METHOD TO ACT ON YOUR VALUES
### STEP 1: FAMILIARIZE

*Assess and prioritize your values.*

The first step is to get familiar with your core values. As I mentioned in chapter 4, everyone gravitates to a universal set of values, but what's most important to you? I value respecting colleagues, equal pay, and zero discrimination along with other values such as compassion, honesty, loyalty, and fairness.

Think of your core values as bright lines that you will not cross at any cost. For me, I will not let a direct report go without properly evaluating and determining if he or she is the right fit for my team. This is about fairness and

---

2   Brainy Quote, "Edmund Burke," accessed August 22, 2016 (http://www. brainyquote.com/quotes/quotes/e/edmundburk377528.html).

respect. This is a bright line for me because I have seen too many managers do this in front of me.

Now that you've thought about your core values, grab a napkin or scrap of paper and a pen and write down your top five. Then flip the sheet over and prioritize them. These steps require strong introspection on your part, so dig deeply and scrape away any cultural hinges, societal strings, and social nuances that have influenced you negatively over the years. Your aim is to strip away any values that were formulated and conditioned by any toxic attachments.

A word of caution: choose wisely. Make sure the values you select are ones you can't possibly imagine walking away from. Whatever you choose to act on will impact you and your career. Just because I value friends and fine food doesn't mean I'll prioritize fighting for good food in the cafeteria over equal pay between men and women.

If you need help recognizing your core values, return to chapter 4 and look at what other leaders have said matter to them. See if any of those values ring true to you.

## STEP 2: IDENTIFY

*Determine the degree of "congruency" with your values and your company.*

Once you recognize your core values, you need to honestly assess if they align with the values embraced at your company. Look at the company as a whole, your team, your division, and especially your boss and leaders. Do you share similar values with them? Are there gaps between what's important to you and what's important at the company or within the leadership team? It's one thing for a company to list its values in a conference room and to post them at the company website. It's another to live by them.

As Lisa Felice, PhD, organizational psychologist and consultant, shared with me, "The organizational values dictate to members of the organization what behaviors are expected of them. Without organizational values, people who work in the organizations will follow their individual value system. It's important to note there are espoused values and practiced values. Espoused values are what the organization promotes. What they say and practice highlights the degree of congruency."[3]

For example, if you work in a boiler room stock brokerage firm with everyone obsessed with money and driven by

---

3   Felice, interview.

greed, but you're looking for honesty and integrity, then you're probably in the wrong place. Attempting to act on your values in a company like this will be like trying to paddle your canoe up the Niagara Falls on a daily basis. It becomes challenging! If you find yourself in a similar situation, perhaps it's time to look for a new river.

Or maybe your values don't match your manager's. Are there other managers in your organization or other teams where your values better align?

It's not always easy to determine how your values and those at a company align, especially when you're fresh out of your MBA program or looking for another job. I've found it helpful to first understand the industry, whether it's financial services, consulting, engineering, technology, or another field that you're in or that you want to go into. Next, research articles written about the company or go to chatrooms with former or current employees who can tell you about their experiences.

A heavy premium is placed in the business world on your network, so tap into it. Ask people you know if they've heard anything about the company. Or try talking to someone who currently works at the company you're eyeing or has previously worked there. If you're coming out of an MBA program, then take advantage of your alumni network to find out the inside scoop on a company, leader, or manager.

## STEP 3: BEWARE

*Gauge the level of toxicity in and around you.*

Once you know your core values and have compared them to your company or team/division, it's time to beware (or be aware) of the toxicity level permeating your environment. The best way to evaluate the negativity in your office is to watch your own behaviors and those of your colleagues, managers, and leaders to see how they treat you and one another. Do they exhibit the four behavioral diseases—deception, detraction, discrimination, and doubt? More importantly, are you beginning to exhibit these four damaging behaviors that I outlined in chapter 3? Or are people on your team treated with respect, compassion, dignity, and other core universal values?

Do the simple task of researching company statistics (e.g., diversity ratios, attrition rates, employee satisfaction numbers, etc.) to better understand the culture within your company. Do you know who serves on your company's board of directors and their key initiatives? Look into the people sitting on the board and their goals, which will give you more insight into the values and priorities of your organization. With this information in hand, you can compare it with the real-life actions and behaviors that you witness daily.

Also, look at the CEO and the executive team to see what values they stand for and how long they've worked at the company. Quick and frequent turnover of leaders can signal something is off in the organization. Have recent publications or the media written stories on your CEO and leaders? If yes, what was said about them? Do they regularly use the four behavioral diseases when interacting with staff or one another? These questions can help you better determine if you're working in a toxic environment.

Another helpful avenue is to compare and contrast your current environment with previous employers. Tap into your friends and colleagues to ask them about their work environments. This knowledge gives you a wider perspective. Sometimes it's difficult to understand if something is toxic without any comparison. Perhaps the level of toxicity you experience isn't as severe as your friends' or maybe it's more severe.

Your work environment doesn't have to be toxic. You don't have to endure bullying or discriminatory behavior from your colleagues, managers, or leaders. Too often, we isolate and justify how we're treated, believing that's just how it is in business. While it's true that some leaders thrive and rule acting from anger, greed, and ignorance and using the four behavioral diseases, that isn't true for every leader or company.

Being aware is as much about understanding that healthy environments exist, too, and that you can work in those companies. "You can still be productive within a toxic environment," explains Robin O'Connell, executive VP at Uphold Incorporated, "but it's like pushing against a strong wind. You expend more energy to go the same distance. You won't necessarily fail working in a toxic environment, but other environments exist."[4]

In figure 2, I show examples of the toxicity levels at a company. This is a good graph to leverage when you compare companies within the same industry that are also similar in size and revenue. For example, if you are in the automotive world, then you'd compare companies such as Ford, GM, and Toyota. If you are in the technology world, then you'd group together companies such as Google, Microsoft, and Apple. Intuitively, you'd want to work at a company with the smallest area box. Granted, these will fluctuate and are subjective in nature. However, it is a nice tool to use as you begin to assess and choose where you want to be in the future.

4   O'Connell, interview.

"Beware of your environment" is a crucial step because it will signal to you the choices and eventual actions you'll need to make to navigate your situation.

FIGURE 2

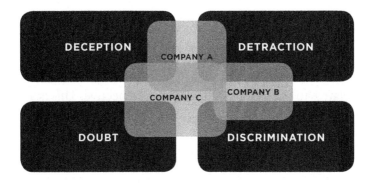

## STEP 4: ELEVATE

*Seek greater perspective internally and externally.*

In Buddhism, the law of karma says the results of our actions will follow us like shadows across our lives. If you harm someone, then you'll be harmed. If you're kind to someone, then you'll receive kindness. That's how karma works. Buddhists believe we pay more attention to our choices and actions when we integrate the law of karma into our lives.

A similar concept applies in our professional lives. If we want to change our experiences and rise above the toxic environments at our companies, we must accept that the only control we have is over our own actions. This step requires mindfulness. It is about assessing your situation and asking how you want to act.

As I explained in chapter 4, you want to aim to be the camera on the tripod accessing all of your vantage points in a balanced way. Step out of yourself and watch the room move relative to you giving yourself new perspective. This is an opportunity for taking on a new mindful approach to being in your environment. This allows you to explore the consequences associated with how you manage the situation, which will give you greater insight into how you want to act.

If you're faced with a lot of discrimination or detraction, you can respond in kind with discrimination or detraction. Or you could choose to elevate above the behavior and act with wisdom and compassion. The question you need to answer is, what will drive greater impact and long-term results?

Or maybe you decide to remain silent for the moment. Choosing not to act is still a mindful decision. You could also decide to look for a position at another company if the toxic environment is too destructive.

All choices have benefits and consequences; there is no universal right or wrong answer. It's up to you to honestly weigh the ramifications of each decision and choose the course that is best for you. Whatever you decide—to stay and conform to the group, to stay and break free, to remain quiet, or to leave the company—the answer largely depends on your core values.

The key is to make an informed decision. Elevating yourself gives you that unique perspective of looking at the situation from all angles and vantage points. This requires discipline and daily practice. Leverage your mind as a filmmaker would to take control rewinding, forwarding, playing the film in slow motion, and hitting the Pause button when necessary. Most important of all is editing your thoughts and approach in real time.

## STEP 5: RELEASE

*Make a choice: stay, stand, or leave.*

In this final step, you have three choices: (1) stay in the toxic environment and continue acting the way you have, (2) take a stand and act on your values, or (3) leave.

There is no right or wrong answer that tells you how to respond. It truly is about what's best for your life and situation.

## FROM BANKER TO BROADCASTER
## CRUSHING GREED WITH FIBER

I met Brian Rose when we worked at the Ford Motor Company as engineering interns almost thirty years ago. At the time, Brian was going to MIT, and he had the opportunity to become a trader on Wall Street once he graduated. In those early days, Brian was all about making money—lots of it.

"I was taught that a man is judged by his business, by his success, by the amount of money he makes," says Brian. "Connecting with my fellow humans, putting others first, and giving back to society was considered foolish."[1]

Brian's awakening happened twenty years later as he overlooked the Swiss Alps in a dazzling chalet owned by Sir Richard Branson. The room was filled with men who were world class in their fields and educated at the most elite universities in the world. Brian's ski weekend featured the most powerful traders from the biggest banking institutions on the planet: Goldman Sachs, Bank of America, JP Morgan, and Deutsche Bank.

Brian was close with these men both professionally and personally, but he found himself lost in their company as their actions always tugged on his core values. Brian amassed great wealth, yet something was missing.

"Each year, I waited patiently for my happiness to follow suit, but it never did. The more money I made, the more miserable I became," he recalls. "Excessive greed was killing my own happiness."

"A man *is* what he consumes—period. Turn on any television station to learn that lesson. These societal strings and social nuances, as you say, are what begin to form us at a young age. They begin to recode our behaviors. Early on, my software had been running my hardware into the ground. I was failing

---

1  Brian Rose, interview by author, May 28, 2016.

as a human being, and I needed to find a new operating system fast."

At forty years old, Brian hit rock bottom and "elevated" himself by walking away from everything. The trips to Monaco, the lavish dinners in London, and the helicopter golf trips were replaced with webcams, microphones, and a YouTube channel. Brian began to do something incredibly different than what he was taught. He began to record and broadcast conversations with people who had great lessons to teach the world.

Thus, London Real, the popular podcast, was born.

Brian's simple rule for his show is that the people he features must have helped others to live a more fulfilling life.

Creating London Real was Brian's way to return to the man he wanted to be and once was. To do this, he had to unlock his code and to be true to himself by acting on what he valued most in life. One of his core values that he had buried was his need to connect, help, and contribute to something that was bigger than himself.

As he returned to his core, incredible people and events began to enter his life.

"It was almost as if the world had been on hold, waiting for me to emerge from the cocoon of my own grandeur," he remembers. "As soon as I did, the universe opened up before me with a tidal wave of positive energy. It had been there waiting all along. I just could never see it."

Every month, London Real is watched by millions of people across the globe. Brian has hosted politicians, celebrities, entrepreneurs, and executives of large companies, but his purpose, which grew from remembering and acting on his values, remains the same: helping others.[2]

---

2    Ibid.

I've made each of these choices at some point in my career. I've stayed in toxic environments. I've chosen to leave jobs. I've taken a stand for my values in other positions. Once I worked at a company I really enjoyed, but certain people lied and took advantage of me personally and professionally.

I didn't want to leave the company; I loved it. So I chose to voice and act on my values. Yet no one listened. They were too busy climbing their own Matterhorn. Ironically, my greatest learning came from the few who abused me at the company because I began to see a bit of myself turning into them. That's when I chose to elevate and release.

I realized the best option for me was to leave. So I did.

I handed in my resignation letter, and immediately, I felt liberated from the poisons of anger, greed, and ignorance. I leaned on my core values, which gave me the strength to take on the fear and uncertainty that was to come. The golden handcuffs that shackled me to stock options, debt, and career promises vanished. In that moment, I stepped out of a cage that I'd locked myself into years earlier. I released the toxic environment surrounding me, and I haven't looked back since.

Other people make different choices. "I've had direct

reports say one thing to my face, and something else behind my back as they tried to make me fail," says Rick Wong, former VP at Microsoft. "I knew what they were doing, but there was nothing to be gained by playing their game. I chose to act and be true to myself, and that helped me, and others on the team, to rise above the toxic environment."[5]

Despite appearances, you're not caged into a situation, regardless of how toxic it is. "People live with negativity, pain, and suffering every day," says Joe Gullo, business leader at Rambus, "because they hate where they are, their bosses, their coworkers, and the industry. In life, this is all optional. Everyone has choices. If you want to suffer, then accept that's your decision and move on. Otherwise, take the high road and don't stoop to toxic behavior. Maybe it's naïve of me, but I still believe there are rational people at the highest levels of a company who will see your value over time."[6]

Whatever you do, don't lose hope. Even if you feel compromised or caged by fear, an overpowering manager, or by the corporate golden handcuffs of stock options and promised promotions, you can still break free. And if you've started to act on your values, but you still feel the pull and

5   Wong, interview.

6   Gullo, interview.

influence of the toxic environments and people around you, that's OK. Healthier environments do exist, but it may take some time and sacrifice before you can access them.

"I'm all for people working and creating very positive environments where human consciousness can flourish and where individuals can flourish," says Sandra Sucher, professor of management practice at Harvard Business School. "But I don't underestimate the challenge of extracting yourself from a negative situation and trying to find a positive one. It's easy advice to give but hard to follow through on."[7]

Professor Sucher explains that there are many questions that someone must wrestle with if he or she decides to leave a position. "If you decide to leave, does it mean that you have to move to a smaller house? Does it mean your spouse has to take a different job to help support the family if you accept a smaller paycheck? If you quit, then can you afford being unemployed while you're looking for a job that fits better?" she says.

"If you find yourself in one of these blind alleys," says Professor Sucher, "there are ways in which you can free yourself, but it's not without work and it's not cheap."[8]

---

7   Sucher, interview.

8   Ibid.

Regardless of what you decide, FIBER is hard work—worthwhile beyond expectations but hard work nonetheless. It stirs uncomfortable thoughts and emotions because it requires us to walk into the fear. "My values don't align, but I need this job to feed my family" is the excuse I always used to shy away from making the hard decisions.

But always remember that the company doesn't own you. It doesn't own your thoughts, your actions, or your future. You don't have to shackle yourself with debt, false promises, and stock grants. More importantly, don't let a toxic environment created by the three poisons cage you. Remember: you are your own master, and the universe will align with your moral center.

When you reconnect with your core values and act on them, you will find yourself in a new arena sooner than you think. The company obviously made a bet on you, so make a bet on yourself. Trust in yourself by being true to what you value most. Your confidence will start to emerge when this happens, and the fear will begin to dissipate, unveiling our greatest strength: choice.

You have the choice to be true to who you are—whether that choice is to stay, take a stand, or to leave. Once you make a choice, the universe will align with your intent. You will notice new friends, ideas, and attitudes begin to take shape in and around you. Trust in yourself and your core values, and you will be amazed at what comes next.

# CHAPTER 7

# AWAKENING CORPORATE CONSCIOUSNESS

BODHI *DEF*. ENLIGHTENMENT

Strengthening my moral fiber not only brought me out of the toxic environments around me, but it also led me to a bigger discovery: a purpose. I knew my own suffering, and I saw the suffering of so many people around me such as coworkers, managers, leaders, direct reports, business partners, and customers. Everywhere I looked, I saw people struggling to be authentic, to stand by their values, and rise above their toxic environments.

I became driven to help others who have lost their values learn how to reclaim them, so they could more easily navigate, change, and rise above the negativity. I wanted others to know that they didn't have to live by the mantra "It's not personal; it's just business," that it was possible and attainable to live by the mantra "It's business *and* it's always personal."

While I want to see change happen on the individual level, I want to witness something on a grander scale as well. I want to see compassion coexist with capitalism. I want to see compassion threaded into the consciousness of each business and all leaders, so that everyone is treated with dignity and respect inside corporations and organizations. I want profits and humanity to carry equal weight.

I'm a proud capitalist. I believe in creating greater wealth, not only for ourselves but also our families and our communities. I agree with Adam Smith, the noted economist and philosopher, who defines capitalism as a system of social organization by which private money making is its chief end. Smith defended this way of organizing human affairs, not just on pragmatic terms but also on moral ones, upending millennia of religion-based warnings that one should shy away from self-interests and wealth.

In Smith's view, pursuing one's interests to the general

indifference of what happens to strangers is central to national prosperity. He believed that free and mutually beneficial trade does a better job of assuring the general welfare than either selfless sharing or charity does.

The danger is when this idea is taken to the extreme, where capitalism and self-interest is *all* that matters.

"If you go back to Adam Smith and the invisible hand, people have interpreted his work to say, 'Look, if we pursue profits—which everyone does in a competitive environment—then that will lead to overall good,'" explains Nien-hê Hsieh of Harvard Business School.[1] "There's some truth to that. However, this idea has created a way for people to avoid asking and confronting themselves and the company about why they're doing something or what they really hope to achieve. It sets up this idea that we can engage and focus solely on profit maximization, which will lead us to the overall good. But the end result isn't always good."[2]

I'm not a monk nor do I choose to be. Is it wrong for me to desire new things or experiences such as a new sports car, a house in the hills, lavish vacations, or a fine wine? No. I enjoy indulging in pleasures and passions, as one should,

---

1    Hsieh, interview.

2    Ibid.

but not at the expense of others and my core values. As Rick Wong says, "It must be a lonely life to run around every day and only think about how you can make more money."[3]

If our *only* goal is to make money and advance our careers, then we're bound to harm others and ourselves in pursuit of those things. When this happens, we've used capitalism to cripple our value system as individuals, organizations, and society. We can all point to real-life cautionary tales of people and companies who/that took capitalism to the extreme and worked without a connection to their values. All you have to do is pick up and read the most current newspaper or watch the nightly news.

As former Enron VP Sherron Watkins (whistle-blower) said, "In order to flourish, a successful capitalist system— really any system, be it education, medicine, business, or government—must be predicated on fairness, honesty, and integrity. In fact, many scholars describe the capitalist system as a three-legged stool—one based on economic freedom, political freedom, and moral responsibility. A weakness in any one leg and the stool topples."[4]

It's OK to want the finer things in life. It's OK to be a

---

3    Wong, interview.

4    Carozza, "Interview with Sherron Watkins."

capitalist and to want to make money and improve your financial situation. It's also OK to say we want to treat ourselves and the people we work with better. However, we need to foster fairness, honesty, and integrity in the workplace and in capitalism. By returning to our core values and acting on them, we begin to temper the poisons within and reduce the chances of ethical fading from taking hold of our lives again. More importantly, we are better able to thread more compassion into the corporate world, displacing toxic environments with positive cultures, and spurring others to follow our lead.

Now is the perfect time for this to happen. We're living in the dawn of an epoch where acting on our core values to help us succeed in business *is* gracing corporate boardrooms and hallways. And it's only going to continue as the next generation, millennials, climb through the ranks with a different outlook and attitude on corporations and profits.

Millennials (born between 1980 and 2003) demand more than massive profits from the corporations they work for and lead. They want their companies to have a purpose, to place the well-being of people before profits, and to make positive contributions to society at large. Numerous studies have found these men and women want to work for companies that share their values.[5]

One study even found that 50 percent of millennials would be willing to take a pay cut to find work that reflects their values.[6] Amazingly, these employees are willing and unafraid to switch jobs, as often as they need and can, until they find the right company. And the next generation wants to work for ethical companies that contribute positively to social responsibility, whether that's the community or the environment.[7]

"Authentic, mission-driven cultures built around purposes beyond profit attract committed, values-aligned talent that is often willing to work for less in order to align their career values," says Tripp Baird, founder and managing partner of the Builders Fund.[8]

Millennials have also led a shift in buying behavior away from the glorification of consumerism to a more measured

---

5   Deloitte, "The Deloitte Millennial Survey 2016," accessed March 21, 2016 (http://www2. deloitte.com/global/en/pages/about-deloitte/articles/millennialsurvey.html).

6   Cliff Zukin and Mark Szeltner, "Talent Report: What Workers Want in 2012," prepared for Net Impact (2012), accessed March 13, 2016 (https://www.netimpact.org/ research-and-publications/talent-report-what-workers-want-in-2012).

7   Michael Soloman, "You've Got Millennial Employees All Wrong; Here Are the Four Things You Need to Know Now," *Forbes*, January 26, 2016 (http://www.forbes.com/sites/micahsolomon/2016/01/26/everything-youve-heard-about-millennial-employees-is-baloney-heres-the-truth-and-how-to-use-it/#7dc21aa354ee).

8   Tripp Baird, "The Cultural Shift Transforming Business as We Know It," *Conscious Company Magazine*, May/June 2016.

view of what's important in life. According to a report by the Brookings Institute, a Young & Rubicam's brand attribute survey found that a majority of millennials belonged to a segment labeled Spend Shifters. Three-fourths of the Spend Shifters say they "made it a point to buy brands from companies whose values are similar to my own, almost all of them (87.5 percent) disagreed with the statement that 'money is the best measure of success.'"[9]

Given their numbers, millennials will dominate our work-places and permeate our corporate cultures, bringing with them the demand for more than simply profits. By 2020, one in three Americans will be a millennial, and it's estimated by 2025, millennials will make up as much as 75 percent of the workforce.[10]

I graduated from college and went into the workforce in the 1980s when most people focused our attention on profits and making money. Of course that's still important, but already the focus for many employees and leaders has shifted to expand beyond just capitalism. In many ways, millennials represent the convergence of capitalism and compassion, and showcase how both can, and I'd argue will, coexist in the workplace.

9  "How Millennials Could Upend Wall Street and Corporate America," The Brookings Institution (2014), 2 (http://www.brookings.edu/-/media/research/files/papers/2014/05/millennials%20wall%20st/brookings_winogradv5.pdf).

10  Ibid.

"There's a lot of talk about purpose-driven and authentic leadership in many organizations today," says Patrick Shannon, partner at Mercer Consulting. "This is partly due to an attempt to appeal to millennials, which are increasingly a larger part of the workforce. Organizations understand that to attract millennials, they need to provide a broader mission and to try and align with their value system. This shift is changing talent management practices."[11]

Many business leaders have already heeded the call to change and adapt. More leaders at companies of all sizes are placing a greater emphasis on crafting vision statements that declare what the company stands for. They're asking themselves, "What's our company footprint? What do we contribute locally and globally? What are we known for? What do we want to leave behind?" Moreover, they're walking the talk with leaders practicing the company's stated values and acting as positive role models to employees.

Granted, it takes time for more companies to evolve and elevate themselves, but the shift is happening. For example, as we see more global crises occur—for example, earthquakes and hurricanes—certain companies such as Microsoft and Google are beginning to step up to help, not just by offering donations but acting as conscious

11  Patrick Shannon, interview by author, September 28, 2015.

and compassionate companies, offering employees and products for aid.

When the 7.8 magnitude earthquake struck Nepal on Saturday April 26, 2015, killing more than thirty-six hundred people, and injuring more than sixty-five hundred, Microsoft quickly responded. In an effort to reconnect the communities, it mobilized more than one hundred local Microsoft Student Partners and staff, all equipped with Microsoft Lumia smartphones with Skype call capabilities, to provide free international Skype calling for earthquake victims. Microsoft also provided charging stations, Wi-Fi hot spots, and TV White Space equipment to restore connectivity for numerous displaced people and responders, enabling them to communicate with loved ones and access vital information.[12]

Google has a dedicated crisis response team that has helped in various disasters such as the Turkey earthquake, Thailand floods, Hurricane Irene, Japan tsunami, and many more crises. They leverage their own solutions that include the following:

~ Creating a resource page with emergency information and tools

---

12   Google, "Responding to Disasters," accessed May 29, 2016 (https://www.microsoft. com/about/philanthropies/disaster-response/response-efforts/).

- ↝ Launching Google Person Finder to connect people with friends and loved ones
- ↝ Hosting a Crisis Map with authoritative and crowd-sourced geographic information[13]

Companies are realizing that it's time to embed consciousness into their everyday business. This includes addressing toxic environments and corporate culture, as well as helping people and communities, who buy the products and use the services. An awakening is occurring, and it's about doing the right thing for our fellow men and women.

A sense of humanity, altruism, and consciousness is being thread through many company cultures.

Today, various groups such as the International Working Group on Compassionate Organizations and conferences such as Wisdom 2.0 have spotlighted the need for compassion in the corporate world. They've also attracted prominent corporations and leaders to their cause. Leaders such as eBay founder Pierre Omidyar, Bill Ford, Karen May (VP of talent at Google), and LinkedIn CEO Jeff Weiner have spoken at Wisdom 2.0 events. LinkedIn CEO Jeff Weiner says he's on a personal mission to "expand the world's collective wisdom and compassion" and that he

---

13   Google, "Crisis Response," accessed May 29, 2016 (https://www.google.org/crisisresponse/about/response.html).

had made the practice of compassionate management a core value at the company.[14]

The conscious capitalism movement says it's about more than taking care of shareholders; it's about taking care of *all* stakeholders including investors, workers, customers, and others. The movement boasts members such as Trader Joe's, Starbucks, Patagonia, Southwest Airlines, Google, the Container Store, Whole Foods Market, and Nordstrom. These companies and leaders have signed on to the notion that business is about more than making a profit. It's about working toward a higher purpose.

The Tata Group, the Indian conglomerate and member of the conscious capitalism movement, is unwavering: "Our purpose is to improve the quality of life of the communities we serve," it reads on the company's website. "In a free enterprise, the community is not just another stakeholder in the business but in fact the very purpose of its existence," says Jamsetji Tata, founder of the Tata Group.[15]

Leaders across industries, sectors, and countries parrot similar statements to those of Jamsetji Tata. Here's just a sampling:

14  Bronwyn Fryer, "The Rise of Compassionate Management (Finally)," *Harvard Business Review*, September 18, 2013 (https://hbr.org/2013/09/the-rise-of-compassionate-management-finally/).

15  Tata Group, "About Us," last modified March 2008, accessed May 15, 2016 (http://www.tata.com/aboutus/articlesinside/The-quotable-Jamsetji-Tata).

*"If you are lucky enough to be someone's employer, then you have a moral obligation to make sure people do look forward to coming to work in the morning,"* says John Mackey, CEO, Whole Foods.[16]

*"We do not have to win at the expense of others to be successful,"* says Paul Polman, CEO, Unilever.[17]

*"If people believe they share values with a company, they will stay loyal to the brand,"* says Howard Schultz, CEO, Starbucks.[18]

*"Have fun. The game is a lot more enjoyable when you're trying to do more than just make money,"* says Tony Hsieh, CEO, Zappos.[19]

*"If you aren't making a difference in other people's lives, you shouldn't be in business—it's that simple,"* says Richard Branson, CEO, Virgin Atlantic.[20]

As powerful as these words are from successful leaders,

16  Peter Economy, "8 Ways to Lead Like It Really Matters," *Inc.*, May 14, 2016 (http://www.inc.com/peter-economy/8-ways-to-lead-like-it-really-matters.html).

17  Jo Confino, "Paul Polman: The Power Is in the Hands of the Consumer," *The Guardian*, November 21, 2011 (http://www.theguardian.com/sustainable-business/unilever-ceo-paul-polman-interview).

18  Howard Schultz, *Pour Your Heart into It: How Starbucks Built a Company One Cup at a Time* (Hachette, 1999).

19  Drew Hendricks, "20 Brilliant Quotes from Billionaire Entrepreneurs," *Inc.*, April 23, 2015 (http://www.inc.com/drew-hendricks/20-brilliant-quotes-from-billionaire-entrepreneurs.html?utm_content=buffer412fc&utm_medium=social&utm_source=facebook.com&utm_campaign=buffer).

20  Richard Branson, Twitter, March 11, 2015 (https://twitter.com/richardbranson/status/575648638367625216).

they require daily practice to awaken corporate consciousness at all levels within organizations. The Buddha said, "However many holy words you read, however many you speak, what good will they do you if you do not act on upon them?"[21]

As millennial and successful entrepreneur Miki Agarwal said, "I think all businesses will have to be conscious businesses. I just joined the Conscious Capitalism board as one of 18 members. The whole idea is that business will elevate humanity—not philanthropy, not charity, not corporate social responsibility, but conscious business. I think businesses in the future won't thrive unless they have a mission."[22]

Even business schools have started to shift and tackle the larger, more complex conversation around teaching business ethics to MBA students. Once, business ethics was a required class students jammed into their schedules between finance, marketing, and economics—the true grit of running a business. But lately, more MBA programs have begun to look for innovative ways to incorporate business ethics and morals throughout all their course work.

21   Think Exist, accessed August 24, 2016 (http://thinkexist.com/quotation/
      however_many_holy_words_you_read-however_many_you/200792.html).

22   "What Do Millennials Want? These Next-Gen Capitalists Know," *Conscious Company
      Magazine*, May/June 2016 (http://www.consciouscompanymagazine.com/blogs/
      press/100884161-what-do-millennials-want-these-next-gen-capitalists-know).

The Ross School of Business at the University of Michigan is one example of a program that takes seriously its need to train the next generation of leaders to think and act beyond only maximizing profits. The Ross School of Business is home to the Center for Positive Organizations, which focuses on topics such as positive leadership, meaning and purpose, ethics and virtues, and relationships and culture in an organizational setting.

As it states on the website, "Our mission is to inspire and enable leaders to build high-performing organizations that bring out the best in people. We are a catalyst for the creation and growth of positive organizations."[23]

Among the traditional business school courses that it teaches, the Ross School of Business also focuses on showing leaders how to bring empathy, compassion, and energy into their workplaces to enhance the engagement and performance of employees and to inspire them toward greater innovation.[24]

Between the rise of the millennial generation, companies redirecting energy and efforts to make their offices more humane, and business schools preparing the next set of

---

23  The Center for Positive Organizations at the Ross School of Business at the University of
    Michigan, "About," accessed March 4, 2016 (http://positiveorgs.bus.umich.edu/about/).

24  Ibid.

leaders to think beyond profits, it appears compassion and capitalism are well on their way to coexisting.

But when we routinely hear "It's not personal; it's just business" sweeping through countless corporate offices, is this vision for the future really possible? "There is nothing inconsistent with compassion and the fundamental economic premises that capitalism is based on, like free markets," says Sandra Sucher, professor of management practice at Harvard Business School. "The problem is how businesspeople take advantage of the system of capitalism. That's where things go wrong. It's not the fault of capitalism. It's the way people use it."[25]

The Dalai Lama also recognizes the immense benefits of capitalism but also its shortcomings. "When it comes to creating wealth and thereby improving people's material conditions, capitalism is without doubt effective, but capitalism is clearly inadequate as any kind of social ideal, since it is only motivated by profit without any ethical principle guiding it," he wrote in his book *Beyond Religion: Ethics for a Whole World*.[26]

The fundamental flaw both Sucher and the Dalai Lama point out isn't the capitalist system; it's the people working

25  Sucher, interview.
26  The Dalai Lama, *Beyond Religion*, 91.

within it. As Steven Guggenheimer, corporate VP and chief evangelist at Microsoft, says, "Companies aren't toxic; it's the people within the companies that can be but not the companies themselves."[27]

We don't need to change companies; we need to change the people within them, starting with ourselves. This is why it's important for us to act on our values and strengthen our moral fiber. Our values connect us to what it means to be human and to our compassion for one another.

Bringing more compassion into the workplace and aligning with our values doesn't mean we stop making smart business decisions. "People used to tell me if they voiced their values, then it meant they could never fire anyone, or take an action that causes pain for their coworkers," says Mary Gentile, director of Giving Voice to Values and professor of practice at the University of Virginia Darden School of Business.

"Many of our problems stem from not being honest with ourselves and not recognizing that many of the choices we make in life and in business involve creating pain, for ourselves and others," she says. "It's just unavoidable. Saying 'Well, it's only business' is a way to rationalize decisions

27  Guggenheimer, interview.

where the best act for the larger good will have painful consequences for some. This is true, but we can still try to create the least amount pain, and we can try to be *just* in the way we make these tough business decisions."[28]

What Mary describes is capitalism and compassion coexisting. For many people in the corporate world today, I know that this notion of threading consciousness and humanity into our offices may sound outlandish. But then, something has to change. Too many people have felt trapped in toxic environments, forced to choose between their values and their careers. For too long, people have been adrift. They've been poisoned by anger, greed, and ignorance and left ethically numb from the sheer number of unethical and compromising situations they've been placed in.

But things are changing. People are returning to their core values and demanding greater compassion and accountability, both from corporations as well as themselves. The movement has started, and it's only going to grow bigger.

28  Gentile, interview.

# CHAPTER 8

# BEING TRUE TO YOURSELF

——

NIRVANA *DEF*. FREEDOM FROM SUFFERING

As I sat next to a bay window in a San Francisco café, I could hear the cable car climbing the steep hill of California Street. It was a late morning and across the table from me was my younger brother, Dave. I was there helping him move into a new apartment as he began a new journey in his life.

As I dived into my strawberries and yogurt, I began to reflect on the choices I needed to make in my life.

"Have you decided yet?" Dave asked me.

For months, I was fixated on finding the right job that would align with who I was and who I wanted to be personally and professionally. I wanted to work for a company that had a purpose in raising the human condition. I wanted to work for a company that served its community and considered this a part of its vision and charter. I wanted to work for a company that acted on my values such as fairness, respect, and loyalty. It didn't matter to me whether the company focused on technology, manufacturing, financial services, arts, or the sciences. I was searching for a company that was authentic and truly did what the leaders proclaimed.

Don't get me wrong, I wanted a high paying job, a strong career path, a positive team culture, and to live in a great location too. I wanted it all, and why couldn't I have it, I thought?

As I shared in the last chapter, more and more companies are operating for more than just profit. I knew this, and I knew that I wanted to join one of those companies. A new Holocene is truly being created that is bigger than all of us. It's an age where capitalism and compassion is converging. As a strong capitalist, I believe in creating wealth and in the distribution of goods and services by competition in a free market. However, I believe *how* we make those goods and services, and what we do with them, define what we become as a society and who we are as individuals. Compassion must play a role for capitalism to prosper and at the same time, to foster individual and collective well-being.

I knew that I owed it to myself to find the right company, with the right leaders—one that prioritized capitalism *and* compassion—rather than taking whatever came my way. So, I dove in and conducted more research than I had ever done before on various companies. I wasn't just being interviewed for positions, I was interviewing the leaders at various corporations too. This process taught me that I was the one with the ability to choose.

As I shared with Dave, I had found three potential companies that fit the criteria I was looking for, but I was concerned about the sustainability of their conscious company charter. Yes, the companies stood by the sworn missions of profits and compassion, but companies change. I was worried that I would get involved with a company, only to watch as its values erode over time. Employees and leadership teams are in constant flux and the culture can easily sway given the people and team dynamics.

But as I talked with Dave, I realized I was one of those employees too. I was someone who would contribute to the makeup and culture of whatever company I chose to join. It was on me to find the right home, and then when I did, it was on me to hold myself accountable to live up to the company's mission and values. More importantly, it was on me to ensure the company's values aligned with mine at all times. Should the day come when the values of the company have eroded because the people changed, then it would also be on me to first voice my values or find another company.

"Yes, I found a company," I told Dave, confidently. "Even more amazing, I found people living their values everyday."

During my journey of finding and strengthening my moral fiber, I had learned there were many others similar to me: people who believed that doing the right thing, the right way, gave them a greater sense of purpose. They didn't believe it was just business. They believed it was business *and* it was personal.

Even today, I still encounter business people throughout the world whose actions reflect this belief.

When I realized that I was in a toxic work environment, I chose to find a new employer, one with a different makeup of individuals, and one that was more aligned with my values and belief system. Not everything fully aligned but that's okay. Our diverse likes, dislikes, thoughts, and skill sets complement each other. And the degree to which we do align, on the things that *really* matter such as our common core values, has had a huge impact on my overall well-being.

## FOLLOWING YOUR HEART

As I mentioned earlier in the book, meeting His Holiness the Dalai Lama was a life altering moment for me. When my first audience with him concluded, I walked slowly back to the hotel elevators in wonder. How did *I*—an everyday business man—end up in a world of divinity?

It all started exactly thirty days before—it was a late evening and the Seattle rain poured hard all day. I was at one of the lowest points in my life. My health, career, marriage, family and friends, were slipping away from me, and I felt the weight of this loss heavily in my heart. I felt empty, alone, and lost, and so, *very* angry. My emotions had bottled up and the pressure continued to build without having any release.

My chest tightened and my throat closed off. Panic started to settle within me as the full weight of what was happening in my life collapsed on me. I began silently searching for help throughout my house. I had no idea what type of help I was looking for just something, anything, that would ease the pain. I paced up and down hallways, I wandered into the kitchen, then the laundry room and living room, until I found myself standing in an empty guestroom.

My eyes drifted to an old night stand. I opened the bottom drawer and found a small dusty pocket book on the Dalai Lama. Years ago, I had purchased this book on a whim but had never read it. I was never interested in the Dalai Lama nor payed close attention to his story and message. However, this time something inside of me urged me to open the book.

I randomly flipped to page eighty-three where my eyes landed on this passage, "In my own experience, the period of greatest gain in knowledge and experience is the most difficult period in one's life...Through a difficult period, you can learn, you can develop inner strength, determination, and courage to face the problem. Who gives you this chance? Your enemy."[1]

The words inspired and calmed me. For just a moment, I no longer felt alone. And something *awakened* inside of me. I had been so focused on what was happening around me that I wasn't looking inward. That brief paragraph was enough to ignite the idea that it was on me to find my inner strength and to rebuild my life.

1   Craig, *The Pocket Dalai Lama.*

I spent the rest of the night sitting on the floor of the empty guestroom, huddled over this tiny pocket edition of His Holiness' teachings. I finished the book, but it wasn't enough. His words stirred something inside of me, and I became thirsty to learn more about the Dalai Lama. The next day I went to Barnes & Noble and read all the books I could find on the Dalai Lama. His words poured into me giving me an inner peace, hope, and a bit of happiness. And the more I read, the more the pain I had been feeling disappeared. For the first time in a long while, I was starting to remember what it felt like to be me, to be my authentic self.

A week later I sat at a coffee shop with my laptop open in front of me. While sipping my coffee, I did a quick Google search on the Dalai Lama—I was still looking for as much information as I could find on this holy man and his teachings. I was surprised when a simple search showed me that he was going to be at UC Berkeley in a few weeks. Without second guessing it, I tried to get tickets for his talk.

Unfortunately, the session sold out too quickly.

Disappointed, but now eager to see the Dalai Lama in person, I kept searching for more public appearances. That's when I stumbled on another announcement. His Holiness was also going to visit Santa Clara University.

When I first discovered the Dalai Lama was going to UC Berkeley, I thought it was a coincidence. This time, I didn't find the Santa Clara announcement a mere coincidence, but rather a sign that I had to keep following. Again, I let my instincts guide me, and this time I was more fortunate. I was able to grab two tickets, one for me and one for my brother, to the event which sold out in a matter of hours too.

But attending the talk wasn't going to be enough for me. I wanted to meet His Holiness in person, so I reached out to the Santa Clara University event coordinator. I explained to her the personal crisis I was in and that I *had* to meet the Dalai Lama. To her credit, she listened to my story.

"Do you know what you're asking," she said when I was finished with my tale. "This is the *Dalai Lama*."

There was no way that I was going to be able to meet the Dalai Lama she explained, the university had too many other priorities associated to the event. Fielding hundreds, if not thousands of requests like mine, would be unrealistic for the university. There was no swaying this woman, no meant no.

I was extremely disappointed but, nevertheless, still excited to see the Dalai Lama and hear his positive message with the thousands of people who would be sitting next to me.

One week before the event, I received a generic email from one of my hotel loyalty programs telling me I should use my certificates before they expire. Why not?" I thought, so I booked my stay at one of the only two hotels I could use them at in the Bay Area—I ended up choosing the downtown San Jose hotel.

The evening before the event, my brother, Dave, his friend, and I decided to have dinner in the lobby of the hotel. As we were eating sushi and sharing a bottle of red wine, I noticed a monk in a long maroon robe sitting in the corner of the lobby.

Something inside me told me to walk in that direction, so I left Dave and his friend, and approached the monk. As I drew closer, a large crowd had gathered around him quickly forming a barrier between us. There was no way I was going to be able to make my way through that group of people, so I turned around and went back to our table.

But then something tugged at me, as though an inner voice, or my heart, was telling me to turn back around, go see the monk, and this time, *don't stop.*

Normally, I would have ignored this inner voice. But this time I chose to trust it, so I listened, and then acted. With courage, I plunged into the crowd. To my surprise, people began to part left and right to let me by. Not once did I have to say, "excuse me," or try to elbow my way through. Once I stood before the monk, I sank to my knees. There I was on the ground as he sat cross legged on a weathered couch above me. He did not speak English but the interpreter next to him helped me to tell my story.

Forty minutes later, the monk held my hand in both of his, and told me to be here, on that weathered couch, at 7 AM tomorrow morning. "OK," I said, having no idea what I was agreeing to.

It wasn't until dawn that I found out the monk had orchestrated a meeting for me with His Holiness—the very thing I had wanted, the very thing that I couldn't have planned, although I tried.

I—an everyday businessman—met the Dalai Lama because from the moment I opened the pocket book I found in the drawer, I listened to my inner voice, and the universe had responded in kind. I didn't know it at the time, but this was the first step in being true to myself and what I valued once again. We all experience moments when our inner voices—call it your heart, call it your values—speak to us. We don't always listen, but when we do, we are led to experiences that we could never have planned or foreseen.

## BREAKING OPEN TO BREAK THROUGH

After my experience with the Dalai Lama, I came to understand that I had been my own enemy. I had caged myself to what I thought would bring me purpose and happiness—a good education, a good job, a good home. I had become so obsessed with attaining these things that I blindly disregarded how I achieved them. Along the way, I had subconsciously veered away from the core values that we all share, like respect and compassion. Wanting and attaining the finer things in life isn't a bad goal, but when we use anger, greed, and ignorance to fuel our self-interests over another person's happiness then we lose a bit of ourselves in the process.

The Dalai Lama once told me that I was my own master. He was right. And only I had the power to break my samsara, to uncage myself from the mindless wandering, and to strengthen my moral fiber.

For me, I had to first lose everything to see anything. When I met His Holiness that morning in the San Jose hotel hallway, my jar shattered abruptly, displacing everything I worked hard for and who I thought I should be. It took a chain of events and deep introspection for me to realize I needed to get back to my true self. Yes, I was afraid but I began to trust myself to do the right thing regardless of the outcome.

Today, I have been able to practice and act more on my inner voice, because I have strengthened my moral fiber. The result? I have established a better relationship with myself and everything and everyone around me. I am more focused on my health, my loved ones, my friends, and my career. I have learned to *believe* in myself—to *trust* myself to do the right thing, always. I am centered. I know my core values and I act on them. My moral fiber is strong, and I'm living a life more true to myself than ever before.

"Being true to ourselves can be hard because many of us are afraid to learn what we find when we look deep inside ourselves," says Nien-hê Hsieh, of Harvard Business School. "Being honest with ourselves requires self-forgiveness, allowing us to take accountability and make real change."[2]

It is hard to be vulnerable, to go inward, and to ask the tough questions about how we're living our lives and whether we're being true to ourselves. All of us have

2  Hsieh, interview.

demons and emotional poisons within us, just as we have core values too.

Our greatest strength is our ability to choose. We can choose to be silent, to feed the poisons of anger, greed, and ignorance, or we can choose to act on our values in various ways.

We can choose to stand up for what we believe in.

We can choose to leave and find a new job that aligns with our core values.

We can choose to walk into the fear.

We can choose to balance our emotions.

We can choose to strengthen our moral fiber.

We can choose to make a difference in the environments that we work.

We can choose to change our lives.

Choosing the path of living from your core values, of strengthening your moral fiber, takes courage. But when we turn away from courage, we're led to a life of regret, which becomes one of our greatest sufferings.

You don't have to suffer by working or living in a toxic environment. You can strengthen your moral fiber, rise above the toxicity, and live a life based on your core values.

When His Holiness held me in his arms, for the first time I realized that life is greater than just me and my own suffering. All of us suffer and all of us seek happiness as sentient beings. This is life, inside and outside of the office.

We truly are our own masters. And each of us has the power to uncage ourselves, to be true to ourselves, and to act on our moral fiber.

# ACKNOWLEDGMENTS

---

I am eternally grateful to His Holiness the Dalai Lama, whose compassion has touched me and so many hearts and minds with greater purpose, peace and inner peace.

A special thanks to all the business leaders and professors whom I have interviewed and collaborated with for this book. Their stories have been powerful and moving.

I am humbled and appreciative to Professor Samdhong Rinpoche who has graced me with his guidance and wisdom throughout this journey.

Finally, thanks to my dear loved ones for their continued support and blessings. Especially, my mother and father who have raised me with endless love, compassion and courage.

# ABOUT THE
# AUTHOR

---

 **SHAWN VIJ** is an accomplished business leader who has over 25 years of Industry and Consulting experience. He has worked in various leadership positions for Ford Motor Company, Ernst & Young, VISA, Deloitte Consulting, Microsoft, and Intel Corporation.

He holds an MBA from Purdue University, an MS in Engineering from the University of Michigan and a BS in Mechanical Engineering from Michigan Technological University.

Shawn was raised in the Midwest and now resides in the Pacific Northwest.

CPSIA information can be obtained
at www.ICGtesting.com
Printed in the USA
BVOW09s0311010817

490775BV00003B/9/P